BARRY CRUMP

THE LIFE AND TIMES
OF A GOOD KEEN MAN

AN AUTOBIOGRAPHY

Hodder Moa Beckett

Books by Barry Crump

A Good Keen Man (1960)*
Hang on a Minute Mate (1961)*
One of Us (1962)*
There and Back (1963)
Gulf (1964) – now titled *Crocodile Country**
Scrapwagon (1965)
The Odd Spot of Bother (1967)
No Reference Intended (1968)
A Good Keen Girl (1970)
Bastards I Have Met (1970)*
Fred (1972)
Shorty (1980)
Puha Road (1982)
The Adventure of Sam Cash (1985)
Wild Pork and Watercress (1986)*
Barry Crump's Bedtime Yarns (1988)
Bullock Creek (1989)*
The Life and Times of a Good Keen Man (1992)
Gold and Greenstone (1993)*
Arty and the Fox (1994)*
Forty Yarns and a Song (1995)*
Mrs Windyflax and the Pungapeople (1995)*
Crumpy's Campfire Companion (1996)*

*currently (1996) in print

Barry Crump wrote his first book *A Good Keen Man* in 1960. It became a bestseller, as did his numerous other books which followed. His most famous and best-loved New Zealand character is Sam Cash, who features in *Hang on a Minute Mate*, Crump's second book. Between them, these two books have sold over 400,000 copies and continue to sell at an amazing rate, some 30 years later

Crump began his working life as a professional hunter, culling deer and pigs in some of the ruggedest country in New Zealand. After the runaway success of his first book, he has pursued many diverse activities, including goldmining, radio talkback, white-baiting, television presenting, crocodile shooting, acting and numerous other activities.

As to classifying his occupation, Crump insists that, he always has been, and always will be, a Kiwi bushman.

He has published 23 books and was awarded the MBE for services to literature in 1984.

First published in 1992 by Barry Crump Associates

Reprinted in 1996

ISBN 1-86958-397-3

© 1992 Barry Crump

Published by Hodder Moa Beckett Publishers Limited
[a member of the Hodder Headline Group]
4 Whetu Place, Mairangi Bay, Auckland, New Zealand

Typeset by TTS Jazz, Auckland

Printed by Wright & Carman (NZ) Ltd, Upper Hutt

"THE WAY I SEEN IT"

BY

BARRY CRUMP

IF IT WASN'T FOR MY MATE CRAIG HOWAN I
WOULDN'T HAVE WRITTEN THIS BOOK, SO IF IT TURNS
OUT NO GOOD HE HAS TO TAKE HALF THE BLAME.

I SUPPOSE ANYONE WHO WRITES A BIOGRAPHY HAS THE SAME BASIC PROBLEM — WHAT DO YOU PUT IN AND WHAT DO YOU LEAVE OUT.
A LOT HAS TO BE LEFT OUT, MOST OF IT, AND I HOPE THAT WHAT I'VE CHOSEN TO INCLUDE PROVES ENTERTAINING. I'VE TRIED TO STICK TO THE FACTS AND I'VE STUCK 'EM DOWN THE WAY I SEEN IT.

CRUMP

CHAPTER ONE

I was born in our grandparents' house in Papatoetoe, in nineteen thirty-five. The place is still there, I've seen it. Giant Norfolk Pine in the front lawn. Brought into the light of day by Dr Lange, whose own son later became Prime Minister of New Zealand. Our father was big and strong and capable. He came from blacksmiths and bushmen. We lived mostly on dairy farms on the outskirts of Auckland and moved around a fair bit. Just sitting here I can think of nine of the primary schools I went to. We were sharemilkers, but all I understood about that was that our father shared the milking with me and my brothers.

"How did you come to meet up with the old man, Mum?" us kids asked her one day.

"I was walking along a lane near where we were living and he cantered along on a mare he was breaking in and scooped me up and rode off with me," she said. And knowing our father that'd be about right.

They got married and had six kids. Brother Bill, then me, then Brother Colin. Sister Shirley, Sister Carol and then Brother Peter. That's my family, they're all okay, too.

The Second World War was being fought when I was growing up. I was nine when it ended. Our father would have made a great soldier but they wouldn't let him join up, they stuck him in the Home Guard and gave him a broomstick or something instead of a rifle. He wouldn't have liked that too much! There were blackouts and army people and vehicles, and general anxiety about the news that came over the radio, but that was as close as the war came to us kids.

The first car I remember riding in was a 1930 Essex with a gas-producer on the back that burnt things like ake-ake nuts

9

and pine-cones because petrol was rationed. Tyres, too, were hard to get and I can remember them stuffing tyres with hay to get a few extra miles out of them. Quite an adventure to get somewhere in a car like that.

It was a typical farming childhood of those times. Horse and sledge, woodstove and pressure-lamp, herd-tester doing the rounds in a horse and buggy, Aunt Daisy on the radio and Sunderland flying-boats in the air over Auckland. Pukekos in the swamp, pigeons in the puriri, possums in the plum tree, and rabbits, hawks and hares throughout the patchy broken-in paddocks. We had no toys to speak of and our main fun was things like crashing through the raupo, raiding orchards, sliding down the hillsides on mamaku stems, bullroarers, flax darts and damming up creeks and shanghais. We grew up with animals all around us and I've always got on well with them, especially dogs and horses.

Shorts, jerseys and bare feet, baths in tubs and haircuts out in the paddock with the horse-clippers, brother turning the handle for brother as our father cut our hair, short back and sides and straight across the top.

"Next!"

Brother Bill has the tip missing off one of his ears from turning his head the wrong way during a haircut. Permanent trim.

He was a hard man, our father, the hardest around, but I've never met a man I'd rather have been the son of. He was kind of honourable.

I remember when our neighbour's cowshed burnt down. The old man went across and built him a new one in several days, while we put their cows through our shed. He was real good at concrete-work. That cowshed was the first anyone around had seen without leg-ropes. A cow only ever kicked the old man's bucket over the once, and he saw no reason why anyone else's cows should be allowed to do it any more than once either.

Despite being a bit harder than some on his animals, our father was a very efficient farmer. He was a good judge of stock as well. He remarked one day that a calf no more than a few minutes old would take prizes at the Calf Club. Us kids grabbed it, and he was right. Freda won top ribbons at the school Calf Club and again as a yearling at the Kumeu A & P Show.

At that stage we milked only pedigree Jerseys and it would take us two and a half hours to put sixty cows through the shed. They were all fed Tomoana Dairy Ration in the bails, they all had to be started and double-stripped, and all the milk went into testing buckets. We consistently topped the butterfat scene for New Zealand.

Us boys weren't too impressed by any of that when we were rounding up the cows in the dark at four o'clock in the morning, chasing up a cow and standing in the warm place where she'd been lying to warm our feet, and then skipping through the frost to the next warm place.

The milkings were always the same. The pulsing suction of the milking-machines, the whine of the cream-separator, the bawling of calves and the clang of cream-cans on the wet concrete. The squealing of the pigs as they clamoured at the white cascades of skim-dick being poured into their troughs. Then up to the house, fresh cream on our porridge and off to school. Don't be late home for the milking, and no picking the bread on the way up from the gate or you might cop a 'reek under the lug' from the old man. Being dealt to by our father could be quite dramatic, but a clout with the copper-stick from Mum was a joke, bless her.

There were the busy times like haymaking, when every-body had to pitch in and pull their weight. Neighbour helped neighbour with gear, knowledge and work, and the atmosphere would become almost festive. The two-horse mower, chatter-ing along making rows like ruled lines, with the grass curling over behind the swath-board like a green breaking wave. Then the tricky-fingered tines of the tedder, tossing and teasing out the hay so it'd dry evenly, and then the rake, drawing it into long rows across the paddock, ready for the sweep to gather up in horse-high bundles and deposit under the steel grab of the stacker. Us boys worked with the men, and the girls helped the women prepare the food and made sure there was always bar-ley-water and scones under the teatowel in the shade. I was working draught-horses when I was too small to put the collar-and-hames on them.

We had the usual childhood ailments – stone-bruises, cuts, measles, and such. The main remedy for any kind of sickness in those days was a tall thin blue bottle of castor oil. This was particularly effective because most kids would rather go to school than have their noses held and a couple of tablespoons of castor oil poured down their throats. We were also told that white bread gave you soft white bones and roughage saved you from getting worms and having.to be given two tablespoons of kerosene. Oil and kero – the world must have been going car-crazy in those days!

I've always been pretty gullible. Us kids were told that if you went out in the rain without a hat and coat you were liable to get pneumonia – double pneumonia. And if you went out in the sun without a hat on you'd get sunstroke. If you went swimming within an hour of eating you'd get cramp and drown, and if you didn't eat crusts and greens you'd be sus-ceptible to a variety of fearful-sounding diseases, like all your teeth and hair falling out. Bald people had obviously cheated on eating their crusts when they were young kids, and people with no teeth – well!

I must have been still pretty young when a cousin told me that horses always talk to each other when there's no people around. I don't know how many times I sneaked up on tied-up horses to try and catch them talking to each other but I never heard a single word. It's probably not even true. One day I saw the herd-tester's horse tied to the fence having a yarn with our two draught-horses in the next paddock, I sneaked along the hedge to try and catch them talking. The herd-tester's horse suddenly saw me and pulled back, some sacks that were hanging on the fence started dancing around and the horse broke its reins and bolted, and wrecked the herd-tester's buggy.

An older boy told me that whenever they took a photograph of you it took a layer off you, like an onion. I desperately avoided having my photo taken after that because I had this idea that my eyes and stomach would fall out if they took too many layers off me. I admired film actors because it was a wonder there was any of them left. When I saw a really thin person I assumed that they'd probably had too many photos taken of them.

I asked an aunt of ours, who was in a position to know, where babies came from, and she told me that God opens a trapdoor in the mother's stomach. I examined my young sister's stomach and, not finding any sign of a trapdoor, pronounced that she would never have children.

It doesn't pay to check this marginal type of information with adults, you can get yourself laughed at. It's better to keep your mind ajar and wait and see if it checks out.

There was no television when I was young. There were serials on the radio. *Talking Drums* and *Moon Over Africa*. And books – Jack, Peterkin and Ralph marooned on a coral island, living on what they could find in the bush and getting into danger on almost every page. Jack London's *Call Of The Wild*, frozen wastes and huskies and wolves, Hudson Bay and the fur-traders. Up the unexplored Amazon with Colonel Fawcett – naked savages with curare-tipped arrows, and twenty-foot anacondas lurking in the steaming jungle at almost every turn and crossing. Ishmael, braced in the prow of the racing whale-boat, his harpoon poised as they close in on the huge stream-ing bulk of another leviathan.

Mountaineers and submariners, aviators and frontiersmen, secret agents and camel caravans. On safari in darkest Africa. At the helm with the big clipper heeling over in the wind. Diving in the coral lagoon and riding a giant turtle out across the reef. All these adventures on the pages of books. I longed to get out into the world and experience these things for myself.

I spent a fair bit of time in a world I made up for myself. They used to call me Dopey because I was always 'away with the fairies'. Our horse-drawn sledge was a magic carpet to me. The horses became not-there, the bumps were waves and the sledge was a ship loaded with urgently-needed stuff, plunging through a stormy sea. My father would say what the bloody hell did I want to go driving the sledge through all that rough ground and mud for? Difficult to explain a thing like that to our old man.

When I was about eight my father and a mate of his ran a hundred rabbit traps. The rabbits were fairly thick around there and the skins were worth a bit. One day they got me to take their traps out to the back of the farm for them. One of the traps fell off the sledge. I found it on the way back and set it, with some difficulty, on a possum-run through some fern. That night I sneaked out of bed and went out the back with a torch. Couldn't wait to see if I had caught anything. And there was a big grey possum in my trap. The first of more than a hundred thousand of them.

I grin as I remember how I slew and skinned that possum.

I tacked its skin out on the wall of the shed. It was worth about a shilling. This'd do me! I scrounged four more traps and ran a line along the edge of the bush. I enjoyed experimenting with different sets and lures to trick the possums, and I caught quite a few of them. There's a bit of a knack to it.

The hills up the back became frozen wastes, the rain was driving sleet and snow, my furs were beaver and mink, and I was an old sourdough trapper in Hudson Bay. Then we moved away from there and I probably slid into some other dream.

Sometimes we'd get our mum in the right mood and she'd tell us the story about the little boy and girl who lived all alone with their mother. Their father had died and their mother worked very hard washing and scrubbing to get them crusts of bread to eat. Then one day she went out into the snow to look for food, and didn't come back.

The little boy and girl searched everywhere but they never found their mother. Finally they got kicked out of their dingy little room for not paying the rent. They had tuppence left, so do you know what they did?

"No!" we'd say.

They went to the Post Office and bought two penny stamps and stuck them on their foreheads and addressed themselves to Jesus and laid down in the snow with their arms around each other to wait for the postman.... The snow covered them up and when they woke they were in heaven with their mother and father.

She told it with such passion and timing that us kids could only sit there hugging our knees with tears in our eyes and lumps in our throats. She was a wonderful woman, our mother. She had heaps to do, but she always had plenty of time and love for all of us. The only time she favoured anyone was if they were sick or hurt or unhappy. Top people, mothers.

There was music in our family. Our father played the piano and piano-accordion, any song you liked. Mum played piano – *Remembrance*, *Sprig of Lilac* and *Dream of Alwyn*. Our mother's first name is Lily-of-the-Valley, no kidding!

It was my mother who put me onto writing. She encouraged me. I'd already written a short-short-short story in a little notebook and showed it to her, something about a wild stallion. I don't remember her reaction to it, but the next thing in that strand of rope was when we were living on a farm near Clevedon and going to school in Papakura. I was about ten years old. There was a polio epidemic on and everyone had to stay away from school for a while. Among the schoolwork we were given was the synopsis of an essay we had to write.

Neither my mother or I are cheats, never have been and never will be, but we cheated. Well, I did anyway. She wrote the essay, mainly, I think, to show me how it could be written. And I got a bit pushed for time and copied it out onto my pad and sent it in. And it backfired on me. Back at school the essays cropped up and the teacher congratulated me on the excellence of my essay and got me to stand up and read it out to the class. Highly embarrassing, I didn't even know it properly. I had to watch my essay-writing after that because it had to be somewhere near the standard set by my mother.

The last of my schooling was at Otahuhu College. Fourth form, Agriculture. I was only ever a barely-average scholar. Like a lot of other kids, I suppose, I just wasn't interested enough in most of what they were trying to teach me. I worked in a woodworking factory when I wasn't at school, a shilling an hour, and paid off a pushbike at ten bob a week. As soon as I was fifteen (slightly before, actually) I quit school and cycled off with a bit of gear in a sack to a job on a dairy farm a few miles south of Auckland. I was out on my own. I'd been looking forward to this for years.

I see that I've skipped through this account of my childhood as rapidly as I'd have liked to at the time. Just as then, I'm in a hurry to get on with the rest of my life.

CHAPTER TWO

The award wage for a farm-hand in the early fifties was two pounds eighteen shillings a week and your keep. The couple I was working for treated me like a son and we became good friends. We were only milking about seventy cows and in between and after milkings my boss and I would go out shooting and fishing. He taught me how to use a shotgun and a trout rod, and signed for my first .22 rifle, a single-shot. He wouldn't let me have a repeater because he reckoned a single-shot makes a better shot out of you. He was right.

I spent nearly all my wages on ammunition, two and sixpence for fifty bullets. I was going through about a thousand rounds a week at one stage there, mostly at targets and tins and stones down by the creek. The hills we roamed around with the shotgun, the .22 and the boss's English Setter, shooting pheasant, duck, quail, pukeko, possums, rabbits, hares and pigeons are now covered with houses and factories and roads. Abundant hills to the south of Auckland!

I could have stayed on that job as long as I liked, I suppose, but it was too easy. This was a stepping-stone to me. I was sick of milking cows, I'd decided to be a deer-culler. The red deer in the back country had become so numerous that the government was employing teams of men to just go out and shoot them. I applied by mail to the Noxious Animals Division of the Internal Affairs Department and they sent me some information and said they'd let me know when they were employing hunters.

I couldn't resist the offer of a job driving a team of horses in bush and scrub country further south, and I moved in with a family who were managing the property. Within a couple of weeks I'd bought two dogs off passing hunters and had caught two small pigs with them. I liked this pig-hunting.

Freedom from the discipline of having to milk a herd of cows twice a day was delicious. I didn't mind how much work I had to do because when it was done it was finished and I could see where I'd been. It didn't have to be done again in a few hours.

This was more like fun to me. I'd get up in the morning and feed my six horses chaff and oats, up to the house for breakfast, back and harness up, put them in the chains and off to work. I'd always been handy with horses and these were easy to manage. They were being worked regularly and each had his or her place in the team. They were a big, gentle, powerful unit, and once the inside horses were settled down and following the last furrow I just had to sit on the discs and listen to them slicing through the fern-roots and churning aside the earth. In the finish I could work them higher up the sides of the ridges than they'd planned to go.

The family I was working under were pleased to have someone who could handle the horses and look after the place, and they started spending a lot of the time at a place they had in town. The boss came out every few days to bring horse-feed and supplies and keep an eye on what I was doing, otherwise I had the valley to myself most of the time. I'd work like one thing for a few days then take a few days off for hunting.

The poundkeeper in town used to bring us out any dogs that nobody wanted but might be okay as pig-dogs. He didn't like them having to be destroyed. This time he arrived with two of them, a soft-looking black and white bitch and a big yellow raw-boned thing called Fred, with bleak yellow eyes and a split ear. He was about six or seven years old. They were going to 'put him down' for having bitten one too many postmen. I sent the bitch back with the poundkeeper and promised to give Fred a tryout on pigs.

The first thing Fred did was saunter over and give my big holder a good shake-up on the chain, and drove the other dogs into the backs of their kennels. I got a chain round his neck, a plough-chain, and tied him to a post in the hedge and fed him the rib-cage of a goat. I could see he was going to be a handful, that dog, but I couldn't have imagined how much of a handful. I believed I had the upper hand because I had a rifle and Fred didn't. I was mistaken.

The area was heavily hunted. There were a lot of big old boars around that were easy enough to get onto but a hell of a hard to stop. They'd survived by cleaning up packs of dogs. In those days a basic pack of pig-dogs included a finder-bailer; a dog that went out and found the pigs and barked at them until you got there with the two holders which were usually at least half-bulldog. The holders would go in and grab the pig by an ear each and you'd go in and stick it and you'd have your pork. No rifles in those days, just a pig-sticker, a cut-down bayonet or something similar. You'd be lucky to catch a pig with dogs like that these days, they've evolved into a more flighty, running animal and they only bail-up when they have to. But this dog Fred I'd come into possession of was ahead of his time. He'd knock 'em up and spin 'em round and hold all comers, regardless.

The first time I took him out we got onto a big ginger boar on a ferny ridge and he bailed-up in a little clearing and dared the dogs to go near him. Fred was aloof from the other dogs, who gave him a wide berth. He was sloping along behind me, he'd probably never seen a pig in his life, but when we came to where the other dogs were furiously bailing the boar he took one look and trotted across and grabbed it over the back of the neck.

Me, the other dogs and the pig where all momentarily stopped in our tracks, this new dog wasn't playing by the rules.

21

Then the boar went mad and started chucking Fred all over the place. He got flung off and landed on his back in some fern and lost his temper. He'd already been ripped in the shoulder. He came up out of there snarling like a lion and flew straight into the boar and they stood there ripping and tearing at each other, both up on their hind legs at one stage. The other dogs got into it and I was able to sneak in and hamstring the boar and when they'd nailed it I stuck it behind the shoulder.

We all knew about that boar, it had killed two of our mate's good dogs the winter before and at least two others we were sure of, and Fred had stopped it on his own, his first pig. It had nearly stopped him as well. His head and neck and chest were a mess of blood and torn skin and flesh. I tied my shirt round his neck to stop some of the bleeding and carried him down to the truck.

He was getting pretty weak by the time I got him home. He let me put him on the kitchen table and clean him up, which took about two hours. I remember putting an extra stitch in one of his cuts where it wasn't really needed, to make it up to fifty stitches. Waxed thread and a darning-needle. Then I went out with the lamp and got some fresh milk out of the cow for my champion pig-dog.

He came right. Many times. Fred didn't mind grabbing a half-grown pig or a sow and chewing into the back of its neck until it suddenly stopped squealing, but if there was a decent boar around he'd run right through a mob of other pigs to get at it, and wade straight into it before it could figure out whether to take off or not. And he took some terrific punishment, even though the other dogs were getting bolder and taking some of the weight off him, and seeing him getting carved up like that sometimes made me go in with the sticker where I normally wouldn't have been game to.

I tried pulling a piece of car-tube over Fred's neck to save him getting ripped, but it almost got him killed when a boar got its tusk and grinder hooked up in it. I was stitching up scars onto scars, but we were getting those boars. It was exciting hunting.

I had to adjust my working pattern to fit in with Fred. When he was recuperating I kept working the horses until he came right, then I'd hunt until he got ripped up again. The boss did all right out of the arrangement, sometimes the dog would have been on the chain for two weeks and I'd only get in two days of hunting before Fred had to be carried out of the bush with his stomach opened up, or gasping through a hole in his windpipe, or a rib hooked out of his chest, or giddy from loss of blood, and it'd be another spell behind the horses for me for a while.

Fred got to be known to the pig-hunters who came out there and some of them wanted to borrow him, but he wouldn't have anything to do with them, or their dogs. He didn't like me much and I'd saved his life half a dozen times. He hated everyone else. Most dogs won't fight a bitch, but not Fred. Dog or bitch, if it got too close to him or he didn't like the look of it, he into it! That went for people as well and even I approached him with a bit of caution. Whenever I heard a vehicle coming down the hill into the valley my first thought would be whether Fred was chained up or not.

I've had a lot of dogs since Fred, he was one of the first, but I've never had one that was such a thrill to let off the chain as he was. For one thing you never knew if you were ever going to tie him up again. When I was going hunting I'd shut all the other dogs I was taking in the cab of the little farm truck and then undo Fred's chain off the post and make him jump onto the back. Then I'd wrap his chain around the rear bumper and off we'd go, with three dogs crammed into the cab with me and one on his own on the back. I know it would have been better the other way around, but Fred had his own ideas how he liked to travel and who he liked to travel with – no-one. When we got where we were going I'd let the other dogs out and back up to a tree or a fence, tie Fred's chain onto it and drive away a few yards to get him off the truck. Then I could let him go and we could all go hunting. It was the reverse procedure going home, except that half the time Fred got carried out and laid half dead on the tray of the truck.

It was easier in some ways when I rode one of the horses, it was just a matter of letting Fred off last, so the other dogs could keep out of his way, and off we'd go. The only snag was that if there were any picnickers or trout-fisherpersons or blackberry-pickers or rangers or hunters parked along the road, Fred was likely to dive under their vehicle and wouldn't let anyone near it or come out until I'd poked him out snarling with a long stick and chased him fifty yards or so up the road. I kept a pole snookered in the bush at the Concrete Ford because that was a favourite place for people to park up, and there's never a decent stick handy when you need one.

I got sixteen big boars with Fred before he was martyred. You couldn't really call him courageous, he was just mad, but you had to respect him. Each of those boars had been fighting off packs of good dogs for years. By all rights Fred should have been killed sixteen times, but he didn't get killed by a boar at all. Perhaps what did happen was just as predictable.

Most pig-dogs let off their steam on pigs and are usually quite placid-natured, but not Fred, he got nastier and cun-ninger. Then one night he let a bloke sneak right past him and watched him siphon a tin of petrol out of the drum under the macrocarpa tree (I had the other dogs tied up over at the shed at the time). As the bloke was creeping back past him with his tin Fred leapt out with a roar and into him. He started screaming his head off, gave me a hell of a fright.

By the time I got down there with a torch and a rifle the bloke was in a hell of a mess. Fred had him on the ground and his clothes were torn and muddy and covered in blood. It looked worse than it actually was because a rip I'd stitched up under Fred's jaw that afternoon had opened up and he was bleeding all over the place as well. I levered him off the bloke's thigh with a horse-shoeing rasp I kept on the post to tap the dog away while I poured milk into his cream-can lid, and dragged the bloke away from him. I took him up to the house and cleaned him up.

Looking back I realise that the poor bloke must have been in shock. He was reasonably badly bitten around the legs and arms and I had to tear up one of the sheets to bandage him up with. Then I gave him a mug of tea and drove him along to his car with his can of gas.

I'd have thought that bloke would have been grateful to me, but he apparently wasn't. He reported Fred to the police. Two days after it happened a sergeant and a constable arrived down the shed where I was shoeing horses. They'd had a report that I had a savage dog here. The complainant had received injuries requiring seventeen stitches.

Seventeen stitches didn't seem all that much to me, and Fred himself would have thought even less of it, but they hadn't come all that way for a joke. They were quite ready to destroy the offending animal. I told them what had happened and it seemed that the complainant had neglected to mention to them that he was on our place swiping petrol and the dog was on the chain at the time.

"Well in that case there's not much we can do about it," said

25

the sergeant. "If the dog was on your property and tied up there's no case against you. Where is it anyway. I suppose we'd better have a look at it now we're here."

"Over here," I said and took them across to where Fred was chained up. He stood there looking at us with his bleak yellow eyes. He never wagged his tail in all the months I knew him.

"Ugly-looking brute, isn't he," said the sergeant, reaching out and patting Fred on the top of the head with three fingers. "What are all these scars?"

"Pigs" I said, pointing to the row of tusked jaws on the branch of the macrocarpa tree.

"Well," he said, turning away from the dog, "As long as he's kept tied up I suppose it'll be all right, but if we get any further complAAAGH!"

He hadn't moved quite far enough away. Fred got him by the back of the thigh, and when Fred bites he doesn't just bite, he shakes and tears as well. The sergeant was on the ground and copping one in the arm before I could get the shoeing-rasp to work and free him.

The Sergeant wasn't grateful. The sleeve of his coat had absorbed most of the damage to his arm and the cuts in his leg were hardly going to need stitching at all, but two stitches in the leg of a policeman was more than equal to seventeen stitches in the leg of a petrol-thief, and regardless of the fact that the dog was on our own property and chained up in front of the most reliable of witnesses, they made me put another chain on Fred and taking a chain each they dragged him down to the river and shot him. Three shots. Poor Fred.

Fred was among the first of many dogs that have kept me company through my life. I like them, especially good ones.

People were a bit rougher in those times. We used to do things as a matter of course that'd be seriously frowned on these days, flipping cattle for example. We had a few head of beef running on the river flats at that place, and the fences were shot. When the cattle got out on the road it was a hassle. I couldn't use any of my dogs on them, they'd have torn them to bits, so we had to round them up on horseback.

The road followed the riverbank and was very narrow and winding, once a cattlebeast got in front of you it was two miles before you could get past it and head it back. So we used to flip them. We'd gallop up behind them and grab their tail. By this time they'd be going flat-tack, we'd time it until their hind legs were off the ground and turn the horse outwards and flip them into a most spectacular somersault and you'd be past them. The horse I had at the time got real good at that. I wouldn't do it now. We were rougher on our animals and kinder to each other then.

Not long after Fred was taken from us the outfit I was working for folded, and I headed south on a train with four dogs in the guard's van and some gear in a sack. I couldn't have taken Fred anyway, we wouldn't have been able to get him off the train.

I worked at various jobs for a few months, mostly on farms, moving further south all the time, towards the mountains. At one place I bought this horse off a bloke for five quid. A thoroughbred that was too slow for racing. Jet black with white fetlocks, it was a real good-looking horse. It was also mad-headed, a hell of a thing to catch and settle down, it had a mouth like iron, it was inclined to bolt, and it'd take off on you any chance it got.

I rode a military saddle with a sheepskin over it, a ten-foot stockwhip coiled at the pommel, my oilskin tied across behind me like a drover. Thus mounted I got around all over the place, my arms and shoulders aching from holding the horse in. It was the worst kind of horse for a lambing-beat because you had to tie it up every time you stopped or it'd end up back at the yards. It was a toss-up whether it was easier to walk or ride. I usually rode, for appearances. (There was a land-girl working on the next farm and we sometimes saw each other across the valley.) I gave that horse away when I left there and picked 'em on performance after that.

The Kinleith Pulp Mill was just starting up. I was one of the first to ride a train between Tokoroa and Kinleith. They'd just opened the line and I hitched a ride in the guard's van with my dogs. I hunted in the pines and native bush around the central North Island for a while, camping in huts and in the open. Jobs were easy to get in those days, and I was a cheeky young coot, but I still don't know how I landed my next job.

I was running out of money so I applied for a job as a shepherd on a big sheep and cattle station, with a ripped shirt, a split lip, a black eye and four ugly big pig-dogs that had been scrapping as well. The manager took me on without seeming to notice my bruised face and bully dogs. He was more interested in whether I was prepared to camp in a hut on my own out the back of the station. That was no problem. He sent for someone to set me up with supplies and drive me out to my hut in a Land Rover. I was a shepherd and labourer on a big station.

My hut was ten miles from the main station on a pumice road that was always washing out. It was a plain little single man's hut, unpainted, bunk, door, window and woodstove. They would have given me a lamp and kerosene, but I've always liked candlelight. The hut was set in the open near some stockyards not far from a pine forest. The land had been recently cleared and fenced and I looked after six hundred wethers and two hundred beef cattle.

A married shepherd who lived a couple of miles out towards the station lent me a skittery mare and an old stock saddle. I put in a bit of work on my dogs and got two of them barking, and shutting up, to the whistle. One of them I could even put out after sheep or cattle and whistle him off just before he got to them, which wasn't too bad considering he was half bull-terrier.

There was a lot happening on that station and I picked up quite a bit of useful experience. Breaking horses, fencing, scrub-cutting, tractor-driving. There was also plenty of hunting in the pines and scrub-country that was still being cleared. I shot my first deer there, a stupid spiker that practically ran into the barrel of my .22.

I was learning things, and holding my own okay, but I still wanted to get into the real back-country and be a professional hunter. I'd been keeping in touch with the Internal Affairs Department, but I was seventeen by the time I got a telegram telling me to meet a Field Officer in Taihape on October the seventh. No dogs on the deer blocks.

CHAPTER THREE

Having to get rid of my dogs was quite a sacrifice to me. I get pretty fond of my dogs, and you always seem to lose a good one just when he's coming right. I sold them to two fencers for ten quid each. Ouch!

'The Department' had given me a list of the stuff I had to bring, like clothes and boots. They supplied pack, sleeping bag, rifle and ammunition, and food. I was there early and the Field Officer arrived late in a small canvas-covered truck with WILDLIFE on the door and loaded with supplies, and two dogs. Apparently the rule about no dogs on the deer blocks didn't apply to Field Officers. He had two other blokes with him who I found out later worked on the station we were shooting on, Ngamatea, so I had to ride in the back with the dogs, one of which was sick on the sack of potatoes. I wasn't impressed.

Miles of dusty bendy road and through several gates and we were there. We had a base hut at the station. I was supposed to have an experienced mate to go into the mountains with, but he hadn't turned up yet (he never did). The Field Officer said I might as well go on into the block on my own and wait for him. He was pretty casual about it so I presumed it wasn't all that difficult. I had no idea what difficult could get like at that stage.

That night I was issued with the standard Internal Affairs pack, sleeping-bag and rifle, gear I was to become very familiar with and very dependent on for the next few years.

The pack was a green canvas bag, about three feet by two-foot-six, with a pocket at the back and wide leather straps buckled at the bottom corners and tied round the top with a short piece of rope. They were originally designed as a skin-bag for packing hides, but we used them for everything.

You always ended up with a big wet patch of sweat where the pack was against your back. We called them kidney-rotters and carried hundreds of pounds' weight in them. There's a knack in packing them so that nothing digs into your back.

The sleeping-bags were thin kapok things with a slit a third of the way down one side. We called them butter-coolers. A canvas sleeping bag cover was optional, and essential. If you put all your dry clothes on and got into the bag inside the cover you could quite often stay warm for long enough to get to sleep. You usually woke up cold, though. A hot rock or a warm dog in the bottom of the butter-cooler bag was a great luxury. The first shooters who used feather sleeping-bags were regarded as pansies, but we all ended up in them.

The rifles were ex-army s.m.l.e. .303s. As soon as we got one we'd strip two-thirds of the wood off it, the magazine cut-off, the clip-holder, the sight-guards, the sling-swivels, the safety-catch – everything that wasn't absolutely essential. Sharpen one edge of the magazine-spring (in case you lose your knife), put two rounds and a piece of candle in the cleaning-gear hole in the butt, shoot her in at two hundred yards, stick ten in the mag and one up the spout with the bolt half-closed and you're in business as a fair-dinkum government deer-culler, ten bob a skin and five bob a tail and if you use any more than three rounds a kill you have to pay for them.

There were no plastic bags in those days and keeping stuff dry was always a problem. Without fire in the bush you could easily die. In the early days you could still get wax matches, but they had to ban them because they're too dangerous around the pine forests. Empty .44 shells were handy because they fit nicely over an empty .303 shell and make a waterproof match-holder. Some of the hunters used to dip wooden matches in varnish to waterproof them.

Fire has played a very important part in my life. I'll always prefer a good fire to any other kind of warmth. I know that open fires are inefficient and wasteful, but they're alive. A camp is dead until you get the fire going, and then it doesn't even matter if the roof leaks. I've written poems about fire.

I spent quite a lot of time on my own that first season, or maybe I noticed it more. The first few weeks were the worst. I didn't know what I was doing and had to make it up as I went along. I rigged up a disgraceful tent-camp on a beech bushline at a place called The Hoggett and made disgraceful loaves of camp-oven bread over disgraceful fires. I groan aloud as I think of that camp, it was even in a disgraceful place.

There were plenty of deer around, you could run into one anywhere, and it wasn't hard to get two or three a day, especially when they came out onto the tussock in the mornings and evenings. Then I found a track that took me onto the tussocky tops of the Mansen. It was a view I never got tired of. Beech bush running up to open tussock tops and basins. The Kaimanawa and Kaweka Ranges, their sides streaked with great grey shingle-slides, and the cold green Ngaruroro River crashing down through the gorge between them, three thousand feet below.

There were bunches of deer everywhere. I backpacked some supplies up there and camped in an old musterers' hut and started building up a tally of hides in the skin-shelter. It was an eight-bunk hut, malthoid covered with fowl-netting and full of holes and rips. The bunks were sacks spread between pole frames, only three of them still usable. The fireplace was big and smoky, no matter where the wind was blowing from. There was hardly any firewood at that altitude and the nearest water was a tiny trickle about three hundred feet down the side of the ridge that had to be bailed into a billy with a mug.

Among the names and dates written on the hut walls with charcoal someone had written, 'The bastard who built this hut must have been a bloody camel!'

And in another place someone else had written;

Damn the rocks and damn the slides,
Damn the deer and damn their hides,
Damn the rivers, damn the tracks,
Damn the Mansen, there and back.

When the wind roared through the hut at night I knew exactly what that old hunter meant. You could only burrow into your sleeping-bag and hope the whole shaky outfit didn't blow off the ridge.

When I returned to The Hoggett I found that the Field Officer had been and left a load of supplies and a note going crook about the disgraceful state of the camp and saying that he was bringing my mate in next time he came. The note didn't say when that would be. In fact it was some weeks before he brought in my experienced mate and told me to see how he worked out and left us to it.

My new mate was experienced at everything except shooting, walking, working, cooking and keeping his mouth shut. He lasted for two weeks and went back out to the station with the packman-cook from a mustering gang that was working in the area. He'd used nearly a hundred rounds of ammunition and got four deer tails. Ruined heaps of hunting and hides.

And so began a parade of different blokes who wanted to have a crack at this deer-culling caper. No one ever found it to be like they expected, and most couldn't handle the solitude and the living and working conditions. Four of them came and went that first season.

The second bloke they sent in reckoned the altitude was

affecting his balance and making him nauseous. He was nauseous all right. We were camped at four thousand feet and never went above five thousand. I wasted half a day showing him the right track out of there. It's quite remarkable how quickly you find out what makes a bloke tick when he's completely out of his own environment. That one lasted ten days and got two deer for about twenty bullets.

There was a long spell on my own after that, broken only by a trip into Taihape to register our rifles. Three other shooters from the Golden Hills and Boyd blocks and I were whisked into town in the FO's truck. We had plenty to talk about and were looking forward to a few beers and a yarn session in the Taihape pub, but when we arrived in town we found that Queen Mary had died the night before and everything was shut. The place was like a morgue, if you'll pardon the expression.

We registered our rifles at the police station and bought a bit of stuff at the only shop that was open, a milk-bar, and back to the base for the night, and back into our blocks the next day. He was a hard man, that Field Officer. We'd hardly got to know each other's names.

It was the first season for all of us. Two of the others didn't see it out, and the other one, Alan, is hunting still. He's never done anything else, forty years of it. There's a bushman for you. His name is Hunter.

I had the block to myself for a while after that and only saw other people when I took a load of skins out and brought in more supplies and ammunition. Then in the last month of the season two mates came, and went. Both of them highly inexperienced and had to be shown how to stalk, shoot and skin a deer, where all the firewood was and how to find the hut when they were lost, how to light a fire and bake a loaf of bread, even though it was obvious after the first few days that they weren't going to last very long.

The first of them was a big happy bloke called Ned, who was good company and better round the camp than I was. Unfortunately he was no good on the hill. He could cook 'em but he couldn't kill 'em. He was just too soft-hearted. After about a week he began to realise he should have stayed at home with the wife and kids after all. He was a real family bloke. I took him out to the station with me and left him at the Base to be picked up, and took a load of supplies back to the block on one of the packhorses. When I arrived back at the station a few days later with my seventy and Ned's two deerskins he'd gone, leaving behind a loaf of bread wrapped in a tea-towel with a note on top of it. Unfortunately Ned used to smear butter on top of his loaves so the crust wouldn't harden, and the grease had soaked into the paper of his note and made it impossible to read. He'd invited me to visit him when the season was over and I'd promised I would, but all I could read of his address was . . . Rd, Good luck, mate!

My last Good Keen Mate that season was a skinny little bloke called Tommy, who had a rather rare P-14 .303 rifle with aperture sights and a five-shot magazine. And he was a terrific shot with it, he could drop a deer at four hundred yards most times. Unfortunately he was no good round the camp, couldn't walk or work or find his way, and would have chucked it in straight away if I hadn't nursed him along.

There were still small mobs of deer out on the tops, but by this time they were getting leery and wouldn't let you get within range of them. Sometimes I'd stalk a bunch of deer for an hour or more and they'd spot me or wind me and take off before I could get a shot in. It was easier to dawdle along a ridge with Tommy, reminding him to be careful of his blisters or his bad knee now and then, until we spotted a bunch of deer. We'd sneak into a good spot and prop Tommy up with a rest across a rock, and tell him which deer to hit and where to hit it.

"The big grey hind at the bottom of the slip there, Tommy. You see her?"

"Yep."

"Hit her right where her neck joins onto the body at the point of the shoulder. Make sure of her, if we wound her she'll run and take the rest of them with her."

"All right. Shut up," he'd say.

He'd take his time and squeeze one off and the deer would go down as though an anvil had fallen on it. Quite impressive with open sights at four hundred yards.

"Get the stag going up the side there, Tommy!"

Down goes the stag. We could often get them milling and confused and pick off the lot. Tommy couldn't be trusted any-where near a deerskin with a knife, but I didn't mind doing the skinning for half the tally. I could kick the skin off a hind in about a minute and a half by this time. I was doing better for hides and ammunition than I could have on my own.

Tommy couldn't keep it up though. He was getting more miserable and homesick every day. I had to let him go out with the Field Officer when he came in with the horses to bring supplies and pack out the skins. The season had only two weeks to go, no more skinning. They took all the tentage and camp-ovens and heavy gear on the horses and left me only about two hundred pounds to backpack the nine hours out to the base at the end of the season.

Two hundred pounds' weight wasn't an unusual load. As frame packs became available, the Trapper Nelson and the Mountain Mule, we were able to carry more weight. One of the tricks you could play on your mate was to put a twenty-pound rock in his pack for a walk to the next hut or camp or a two-thousand-foot climb onto the tops, but you'd have to know him pretty well.

At a deer cullers' reunion in Rotorua years later they held a back-packing competition and one of the shooters carried over seven hundred pounds of sand on a Mountain Mule pack-frame. That's more than twice what you'd put on a packhorse.

There were only three of us left shooting in the Kaimanawas when the season ended. We were given our cheques and dropped off in Taihape with our rifles and packs and told that if we wanted to shoot the winter we'd have to apply through the office in Rotorua. One of the other shooters had a motor bike stashed in a garage in Taihape and he took off for Napier, leaving two of us kicking our heels in Taihape with less than a quid in cash between us.

It was Friday of a long weekend and we couldn't cash our cheques until the Monday. We were in town for the first time in months, cashed-up and rarin' to go and all we could do was camp in the cemetery and wait until the banks opened on Monday.

We had a bit of a fire going and that's what must have given us away. I woke up in the night with a torch shining in my face and a boot kicking me none-too-gently in the ribs. I got my arms out of my sleeping-bag and grabbed the boot and twist-ed it, and the new police sergeant went down against a con-crete thing and hurt his hip. He wasn't a happy man. He made us put our fire out and pack up our gear and off to the police station in his car.

In those days if you didn't have a trade of some sort it was generally agreed that you were never likely to ever amount to anything, and if you didn't have a permanent address you needn't expect any sympathy from magistrates. They charged you with being 'A Rogue and a Vagabond of No Fixed Abode and with Insufficient Visible Lawful Means of Support'! We called it being On The Vag.

My mate and I were nothing much to look at, and the fact that we had Treasury cheques for hundreds of pounds on us seemed to make the sergeant more suspicious of us. He locked us up until he could check out our story on Monday. We weren't going anywhere till then anyway, but after the hundreds of hours I'd spent up there in the mountains planning what I was going to do when I hit town with my pay-cheque, I found myself spending the first weekend in the Taihape slammer. There was something pretty funny about that at the time and I started laughing. My mate in the next cell didn't know what I was laughing about but he joined in, and we cracked up laughing until the sergeant came rattling in.

"What's so funny?" he wanted to know.

"Nothing," we told him.

"Well keep it down in here or I'll give you something to laugh about."

We'd got off on the wrong foot, as it were, with that sergeant, and the only times he let us out of our cells all weekend was to stack some sheets of corrugated iron and weed his vegetable garden. The only good thing about it was the tucker, and his wife cooked that. On the Sunday night we discovered that we weren't even locked in, but the sarge had our cheques and rifles and packs so we had to stick around anyway.

The next morning the sergeant must have done some ringing up because he came and told us it looked as though our story held up. He was going down to the bank to check our cheques out. We were hoping he wouldn't take too long because we'd cut half his vegetable plants off under the ground when we were weeding them the day before and it was a warm morning. Out of the cell window we could see the plants we'd cut off already wilting onto the freshly-dug ground.

The good sergeant returned, admitted he'd been wrong about us, gave us our gear and cheques, and told us to get out of town on the next bus. My mate tried to demand an apology but I got him out of there and on the next bus out of town before he got us locked up again. He couldn't read that sergeant properly.

I hung around home for a couple of weeks, quite out of touch with what everyone else was doing, then I got word that I had a winter block at Wakarara in the Ruahines, hunting pigs and goats. I rousted out a pack of dogs and went down there on a train, and was met by a Field Officer and a hunting mate called Johnny, who was a real good hunter. He had three Airedale-cross dogs that were hard and fast.

That block was some of the best pig-hunting either of us ever knew. A snow-boundary came down on the Ruahines and the pigs had nowhere to go. We got literally hundreds of them and about thirteen hundred goats. The dogs that survived that season were crackerjacks, both of them. We'd started the season with seven dogs and picked up another seven or eight locally. Some nasty boars down that way.

That's where I got into using working-dogs for hunting, preferably heading-dogs. They're smarter than the bully breeds, lighter on their feet, more reliable, easier to feed and they'll keep a pretty good pig busy till you can get there with a rifle, if they can't hold it.

For the next few years my life was filled with mountains and bush and rivers, rain and snow and ice and sweat. I shot deer in most back-country areas of New Zealand. There were deer everywhere. Most of the men who hunted had been caught up in the war and the only times much of the country was hunted at all was by old-timers, trophy-hunters who usually carried an old Long-Tom rifle with a five-shot magazine. They'd shoot a young hind and hang it up for meat and then wouldn't fire another shot unless they stalked a stag with a bigger head than the ones they had on the wall of the shed at home. Eighteen-pointers were common in those days, though I myself never shot a decent head. We were after numbers.

They were tough old rags, those mountain men. Tea and rice and salt were their main supplies. Imagine what they thought of us louts. Condensed milk, tinned cheese, army biscuits, ten-shot magazines, shooting everything that moved, hinds and all! We were ruining the back-country. Beneath contempt. Pansies!

Despite all the hunting we weren't making much impression on the deer numbers. Quite often there'd be deer standing around on the ridge watching you skin the ones you'd shot. You can only carry so many hides. It was easier when they cut out the skinning and we just had to bring in the tails as proof of what we'd shot. Some of the shooters down south were getting a hundred deer a day each. The deer we were shooting for fifty cents each would later be worth up to three thousand dollars.

There were no huts or tracks in many places, you just had to follow the ridges and creeks and find your way about, and tent-camps had to be packed in and erected, which took a lot of time off your hunting and tails off your tally. A block where you could use packhorses was regarded as cushy.

I remember the names of our packhorses, Hori, Caesar, Rose, The Black, Bullet . . . . Four of them could carry a thousand pounds of gear and supplies for six or seven hours through some pretty impressive countryside and keep it up day after day. We appreciated those horses. Lake Waikaremoana was a real cushy block, you could get around your huts by *boat*!

There was a story going round about a big station down

south where they used sixteen pack-mules to transport stuff out to the back of the property. It was a three-day trip and their new packman, a Maori bloke, was cutting half a day off it. It had them puzzled until they discovered that he wasn't unloading his mules at night so he wouldn't have to spend two hours loading them up again in the morning.

Our Field Officers were all experienced bushmen who could handle a bit of paperwork. It was their job to sort out the men who could take it from those who couldn't, and they usually did this by sending them into a vast tract of mountainous bush and leaving them there. You can't tell by listening to a bloke or looking at him whether he's going to be any good in the bush. Big muscular men are often useless, and stringy little blokes are often top-tally men, but not always.

If you wanted to check out a new shooter they'd sent in you'd take him into a valley somewhere he didn't know the way out of and leave him camped there on his own, telling him you'd be back in three weeks or so. It's the first time in his life he's been completely out of touch with other people. Three or four days is usually enough to leave them alone. You can tell straight away whether they're shooter-material, if they're not they'll only want to know where the nearest road is. It's the kindest way.

During my second deer season some of the shooters, including me, had to report to Rotorua to have a medical test for a thing they had going called Compulsory Military Training, where any bloke who got to eighteen had to do three months in the army, in case they got us into another war. This was particularly inconvenient to us shooters because three months off your block would completely ruin your chances of getting any sort of a tally for the season.

It must have been inconvenient for quite a few other people

as well, there were blokes eating balls of silver paper so they'd show up like ulcers on an x-ray. Some ate spoonfuls of nutmeg because there was a rumour that it made your heart flutter. Those medical examiners must have heard some pretty ingenious stories, including mine. Such were the warriors of the fifties. And most of them ended up in the army, and it did them a heap of good, from what I could see.

It might have done me a heap of good too, only I'd had the army thing laid on me at high school and I wasn't going to be in it. I'm still glad I didn't have to resort to my B, C, or D plans, which included faking an accident in the Whirinaki Gorge and shooting through to the South Island and hunting under a bodgie name, pretending to be a lunatic, which I wasn't bad at, or stocking up on ammunition and holding out in the bush.

Fortunately my A plan worked. I made out I was as keen as mustard to do my army training, I was actually thinking of making a career out of it, sir. But I was unable to conceal the fact that I was almost totally deaf in one ear and marginal in the other. They regretfully classed me as unfit for military duty on medical grounds, and I got on with shooting things other than people.

Knives are worth a mention. Most of the bushmen, hunters and shepherds carried a sheath-knife and steel on their belts, but we'd given this up as unnecessary weight to cart around. We found that one of those ordinary stainless-steel kitchen knives were all you needed. Sharpened up they'd hold a good edge all day and you didn't have to carry a steel around with you all the time. One bloke I shot with started the deer season with a kitchen knife that had been filed down so often that there was only about three inches of the blade left on it. It was all you needed to tail a deer, token a possum, stick a pig or

43

bone out your meat. If you wanted to cut a slice of camp-oven bread you could always use the slasher.

A bunch of us who shot the Urewera Country in the mid-fifties have remained friends ever since. There was a different attitude towards the bush in those days. It was hard to believe we could have made a significant difference to it, there was still so much of it left. Native timber was still being felled and milled and burnt off. We thought nothing of blazing a two-foot row of chips out of both sides of a tree with an axe to mark a track, or dropping a big rimu with a bag of spuds in a supply-chute caught up in its top branches.

The bushmen used to tell how they'd go through a whole face of native bush, and scarf and lightly back-cut all the trees, leaving them standing. At the top of the ridge they had what they called a trigger-tree. They'd fell that into the one below it and set up a spectacular spreading ripple of falling trees across the whole face that left hardly anything standing. It was called a 'Drive', and when one 'hung up', which sometimes happened, there was great anxiety until the wind set it off again.

There was a poem around that went;

Jack stood on the jigger-board,
The tree she gave a crack,
It was his only trigger,
And the bastard she fell back.

When the fallen bush was dry enough and the wind was right they used to ride horses along the bottom with burning lumps of pumice dipped in diesel-oil on a long twist of fencing-wire, setting fire to the face. Some of the big trees would burn for weeks. The description 'Still got bush on it' indicated that the land wasn't a hell of a lot of use yet.

The timber towns in the fifties, especially around the central North Island, were wild and exciting places. There were some hard men and women around. They were cutting all native timber, rimu, matai, totara, and single people and families moved from mill-town to mill-town. It was a way of life that vanished with the bush.

Virtually the only social life those people had were parties. There were few pubs and they were always miles away and they closed at six o'clock in the evening, which led to a lot of sly-groggers setting up around the mill-towns. Often the local taxi bloke filled this post. There were some wild home brews brewed, too. Anyone who was around then will remember the parties in mill huts that went on for days. You could hear them from one end of the town to the other and beyond, thumping out *Dear John* or *The Bubbles on the Beer Keep Haunting Me*, their only musical accompaniament an old guitar with a couple of strings missing. One of the songs that always got thrashed at these parties went;

From the bushman to the breaker-out,
From the breaker-out to the skids,
From the skiddy to the breaking down,
From the breaking-down to the bench,
From the benchman to the tailer-out,
From the tailer-out to the yard,
From the yardman to the railroad track,
That's where my timber goes.

And that's where the timber went. As the bush was cut out and the mills closed down, the mill-town people dispersed away into the pines or other occupations and all that's left now are a few overgrown beams and heaps of sawdust and tangles of rusting wire rope lying around the disintegrating skids.

On the extreme south-western corner of our block one season there was a pub. The Rangitaiki pub. It was a hard-case outfit. There was a sign saying, RANGITAIKI HOTEL. CROOK BEER, DIRTY GLASSES, SHORT CHANGE, INCIVILITY, and that's what you got. We walked out there a few times, seventeen miles across the plains, and got to know the people who lived around the pub and in the bush at Poronui and Tarawera. We got all the deer tails off the bushmen and the private shooters who came there for three rounds of ammunition each, and we did all right out of it. Twenty deer a week each from the bar of the Rangitaiki pub.

When the deer season ended I gave the hunting a miss and worked in the bush with a mate from Rangitaiki, post-splitting in a block of red beech. He was a great bushman, Norm. One of the old breed. It was all crosscut sawing in those days, a skill in itself. Chainsaws were just coming into use in the New Zealand bush. The first ones were six feet long, took two men to operate, and were way out of our reach financially.

We rubbed our way through the logs with a six-foot saw that Norm kept perfectly set and sharpened. It drew strips out of the cut, rather than shavings, and you could watch it slice through the wood with every stroke, but it was still slow and heavy work. Sometimes we had to put jigger-boards to twelve or fourteen feet up a tree before we were above the flanges where we could build a platform and put our scarf in and fell the tree. On an average day we could cut enough lengths off a log to split out a hundred posts. At seven pounds ten a hundred the money was quite good, but we were earning it.

Halfway through the winter the bloke who ran our block of bush went bankrupt, owing Norm and me for two truckloads of posts. There was nothing we could do about it, we were the least of his creditors. Norm got a job felling in the native and I joined a gang cutting a track along the top of the Huiarau Range in the Urewera.

46

A few days after I got there two other blokes and I got snowed in for six weeks in a tiny hut on the crest of the range. After dragging the crosscut and swinging the splitting hammer with my old mate for nearly a year I quite enjoyed the rest. It was weeks before the purple stain of beech-sap came out of the skin of my hands.

I'd only worked with Norm for a few months, and known him for only a couple of years, but we became real close. I stayed with him and his family at Rangitaiki when we weren't up in the bush. He paid me a real compliment when he took me under his wing and shared his lifetime of experience in the bush with me.

After he died, Norm's sons, not yet in their teens when I'd last seen them, gave me the old Hytest axe that he used to jokingly say he'd had for twenty years – three new heads and five new handles.

Norm and his wife were part-Maori and they taught me things about Maoridom I hadn't been aware of. It had never concerned me whether anyone was Maori or not. They were brown-skinned and they'd always been around, and they could be good or bad like anyone else. They often had a better sense of fun than pakehas and weren't so critical of other people. Generally more tolerant.

But it was only when I met people like Norm and Grace (how well-named she was!) and lived in the Urewera Country and got to know the Tuhoe people, the Children of the Mist, that I began to realise what a treasure lies in the Maori heart, stifled by the European culture so crudely imposed on it, but still tickin' away there.

To me there's something vital missing from the places in New Zealand, Aotearoa, where there are no Maoris living and singing and laughing. There's still a bit of racial prejudice and other ignorant stuff around, but we'll grow out of it. None of us picked what we were going to be born as or into. We'll wake up to that one of these days.

This poem I wrote a while back says a bit of what I reckon about pakemaoriha.

BATTLE
I haven't lightly undertook
Correction of a history book,
But snugly rests the head at night
Who has that day put someone right.

With trembling hand I undertake
To rectify the grave mistake . . .
Of certain academic flaws
In versions of the 'Maori Wars'.

According to these gentlemen
There's only one thing for it;
A Maori couldn't comprehend
A good thing when he saw it.

I don't know what they seek to gain
By making this suggestion,
The soundness of the Maori brain
Has never been in question.

What fool would turn a bargain down
Like fishhooks, blankets and an axe,
When all he'd known were wood and bone
And all he'd ever worn was flax?

What maniac would fail to swap
Some land for mutton, beef and hog,
When hitherto his only chop
Was bird, or rat, or skinny dog?

Who'd fail, unless he'd lost his wits,
To emulate the wily ones
Who sailed the world in mighty ships
And brought him tomahawks and guns?

And having got these wondrous things,
Who wouldn't want to try them out?
And that's what all the quarrelling
And all the fighting was about.

Any mother anywhere
Will understand the claim:
Give little boys the best of toys . . .
They'll quarrel just the same.

And as the flag of God unfurled
The different tribes across the world,
In deadly clashes such as this,
Attacked each other's prejudice.

In spite of who believes they're right,
Or what men say they're fighting for,
The only kind of war we fight
Is still the same old human war.

So in the broader sense, you see,
The 'Maori Wars' will cease to be,
And future books will only say
That humankind grew up this way.

Anyway, when the deer season started in October I got the Waiau block in the Urewera, a big wide easy valley with open bush and good poaching opportunities. I had a good mate, Bob, and the season was pleasant and easy. But there was something wrong, there wasn't enough happening.

One of the cullers once observed how you'd be walking along thinking about something – and a couple of deer would get up in front of you. You'd shoot them, take the tails off them and maybe a backsteak or two, and carry on – still thinking about the same thing you were before. When I first heard that it was hard to believe, but now it was happening to me, and I couldn't help thinking that when a thing like shooting a deer doesn't break a man's train of thought he's probably done enough of it. I think that might be when I started being con-scious of the waste of tucker involved in all this hunting. I'd never given it much thought before that.

One deer I shot that year has broken my train of thought more than once since I picked him off in the Pohukura. I've never shot a deer head worth carrying out of the bush. I should have run into one, but I didn't. This stag had something better than big antlers, though. He had a white blaze down the front of his face. I didn't notice it until I'd tailed him and it didn't break my train of thought enough to think of bringing the head-skin. I was poaching at the time and got about twenty deer that day, and at the time this was just one of them. I've never seen or heard of anything like that in red deer. I could have just about stuck my own price on that head-skin.

I had the usual number of close shaves in the bush, cliffs, flooded rivers, falling rock, getting bushed and such, but one thing that happened that season really rocked me. I wanted to go down the Waiau Gorge to the Maunganuiohau River. I'd been told that you couldn't get down the gorge to the

Maunganuiohau, which meant you had to climb across a high bluff.

I decided to rock-hop my way down the gorge and see how far I could get. It became all boulders, some of them bigger than the room you're in, with the river roaring down through them. I was jumping from rock to rock and making good progress. Then I saw down ahead of me the grassy flats at the mouth of the Maunganuiohau River, three or four hundred yards away.

I jumped off a boulder onto another one a few feet below me and before I landed I saw that you couldn't get down the Waiau Gorge to the Maunganuiohau River. There was no way I was going to get any further and there was no way back. The next rock was too far away and the one I'd just jumped off was too high to get back up on. And the river was boiling and sucking underneath. This was suddenly very serious.

I've heard how people in times of extreme peril can perform feats of incredible strength and agility, and I think that must have been how I got off that rock. I landed on it, turned and jumped straight back onto the one I'd jumped off. I didn't even drop my pack or rifle. I jumped about five feet across and five feet high with a rifle and a sixty-pound pack on my back and I landed well up on the rock. If I'd hesitated I'd have been a goner.

I didn't mind going back and climbing over the bluff after that. I tried to get my shooting mate to come and have a look at where I'd jumped that jump but he reckoned he'd take my word for it. It's the close shaves that keep a bloke in line.

When the deer season ended four of us who'd been shooting out of Ruatahuna took jobs at Murupara, felling pine for the Kaiangaroa Logging Company, who were desperate for bushmen. They'd come badly unstuck. They were just starting

51

logging and they'd built hundreds of houses and single accommodation and flash facilities such as we'd never seen. Then they'd sent someone to Canada to recruit three hundred lumberjacks and sign them up for three years in return for their fares out here.

They got their three hundred men all right, but none of them were lumberjacks. We never saw one who'd ever swung an axe in his life. There were a lot of alcoholics and perverts and criminals and other misfits among them. A year after they'd arrived there were only half a dozen or so of them left in Murupara.

The bush-gangs were made up mostly of Kiwis, many of them Maori blokes. After felling native bush on steep country we found the pines on the plains real easy going, especially now that we had chainsaws. It was around this time that bushmen like Sonny Bolstead and Rugby Edwards were showing them in Canada how to swing an axe and sling a saw. They could go through an eighteen-inch log with an M-tooth crosscut faster than the Canadians could do it with a chainsaw, and after a few chopping demonstrations the Canadians discarded their double-bitted axes and took up our style of axe. If the Logging Company had sent those blokes to recruit their lumberjacks they'd have saved themselves a lot of money and hassles.

Things were changing in the bush. By this time the Forestry Department had taken over noxious animals control. Tracks were being cut and huts put in everywhere. Supplies were being airdropped, thrown out of an Auster plane with the door off.

Then they brought in a token system for opossums, two and sixpence for the ears and a nine-inch strip down the back. We knew where the concentrations of opossums were in the Urewera, whole watersheds that had never seen a trap or poison-bait. A mate and I threw in the bush work and took a block.

The cyanide we used was in hunks like lumps of salt and we crushed it into powder with an ordinary mincer – and survived. A possum only had to sniff that stuff and he'd drop dead. We frequently got five or six of them lying around a bait that hadn't been touched. The most I got was eleven. I heard of someone getting seventeen off the one bait. We'd put a spoonful of aniseed-flavoured flour beside a possum run and then a tiny dab of cyanide on the top of it.

Taking one side of a valley each, we'd lay poison-lines for three days, up and down the spurs and ridges. Then we'd go around taking the tokens off the dead possums. In those first days a line would get anything from two hundred to five or six hundred possums, if the weather held out on you. My mate picked up over eight hundred off one of his lines.

We had an experience at one of our camps that only my mate and I know the truth of, but I'll tell you anyway. We had a bit of a tent camp on a bush flat in the Manuohau Stream, about five hours walk up the Horomanga River and over a fairly high ridge. We'd taken a load of possum tokens out to Gisborne and were back-packing a load of stuff in to our camp. We had heavy packs, we were using a lot of flour and it's weighty stuff.

On the way in there we were resting in a konini creek-head and suddenly there was a flurry of sound and four deer came running down the gully and jumped over the log we were leaning our packs against. One of them jumped inches away from Dunc's head. By the time we'd struggled out of our packs and stood up they were gone. They must have caught our scent in an eddy of wind.

We were hacked off, we could have used some meat and we only carried a rifle when we were travelling, they're too much nusiance when you're laying possum lines. They were the only deer we'd seen all the way out and back in again. Dunc circled round in the bush to try to get a crack at one of them, which took about an hour. No luck.

It was dark by the time we dropped into the Manuohou stream-bed and we had to fumble our way the last twenty minutes to the camp in the dark. When we got there we found our camp was demolished. We had to light matches and poke around our scattered gear before we could see what had happened.

A mob of pigs had gone through the place. The whole flat was turned over and our stuff was spread around everywhere, chewed, spilt and half-buried in the pig-rooting. The tent was hanging from a tree by one rope.

"Blasted pigs!" I said.

"Listen," said Dunc. "They're still around. I can hear one."

We listened. A pig grunted somewhere right near us. Dunc cocked a rifle and I struck matches and we crept carefully forward until we could see a dark shape move in the flare of a match.

"I'll light another match and you shoot it," I whispered.

I held several matches in a bunch and lit them.

"Hey," said Dunc. "That's my bloody sleeping bag!"

There was a pig trapped in his sleeping bag. We worked out where its head was and donged it with the back of the axe through the bag. I dragged it out and knifed it and dragged it away a few yards. A young boar about sixty pounds.

"Hey," yelled Dunc again. "There's another one here!"

I swear, there were two half-grown pigs in Dunc's sleeping bag. We got a candle out of one of the packs and lit it and dealt with the other pig. And what a mess. The bag was ruined, feathers all over the place. Those pigs had been stuck in there for a couple of days and it stank something terrible.

It took about an hour to get what was left of our camp sorted out. Dunc had to sleep with all our spare clothes on wrapped in the tent after that.

About twenty years later I ran into Dunc down south, still shooting deer, and while we were yarning I asked him if he'd ever tried telling anyone about the time we found two pigs in his sleeping bag.

"No, have you?" he said.

"Once," I said.

And we grinned. It would have to remain our private memory.

We took thousands of possum tokens off that Manuohau watershed. We were making more than a thousand pounds a month between the two of us. We'd have had to shoot a lot of deer to match that. We bought a Land Rover and toured around the country, surfing different beaches, laring up, running hundred-trap lines whenever we needed more money, and generally enjoying life. Did a winter on pigs and goats at Colville on the Coromandel Peninsula, bought a Norton Dominator motorbike and wound up in Auckland, where one of the shooters introduced me to a woman who I thought was pretty beaut.

I still think so. She must have thought I was a bit beaut too, because we ended up getting married. And then pregnant.

"That'll stop your gallop, Crump," one of my mates remarked.

CHAPTER FOUR

We lived in my wife's family home in the suburbs of Auckland. I worked at various jobs but never found one I really liked. On building sites, driving trucks, felling trees for people, landscape-gardening work, trapped a few possums in the Waitakeres – stuff like that. The work was dull but the people I was meeting were interesting enough for anyone.

My wife had a large circle of friends and many of them were writers and poets and painters and architects – even a sculptor. All part of the magic that was happening in New Zealand in the fifties. And here I was, straight off the turnips, chucked in amongst that lot. I hope they enjoyed me as much as I enjoyed them. I can think of nineteen poets and writers I met around that time.

Among my new friends were a bunch of young blokes who were starting up a literary magazine called MATE. It was one of them, Kevin, who talked me into having a go at writing a short story, and they published it. I was a bit surprised at how easy the writing of it was. Kevin had a large collection of books and I soaked them up almost as he recommended them. Caxton, Dickens, Lamb, Trollope, Lear, Mark Twain, Lewis Carroll, Banjo Paterson, Butler, Leacock, Saki, Thurber, Dylan Thomas, Waugh, Kingsley Amis, Joyce Carey, Aldous Huxley, Nancy Mitford, Wodehouse and many others. I can't tell what influence all this reading had on me, though I know I was very impressed by Roald Dahl's short stories, he has to have been one of the very best at it. I enjoyed them all.

As the fifties drew to a close, so did our marriage. My wife and I weren't hitting it off too well at all and our third son was still a baby when our paths parted. No-one's fault, we're still good mates. She later remarried and I'm grateful to her husband for the way he reared my sons along with his own.

I hung around Auckland for a while, not knowing what I wanted to do next. Then I met Jean, a quite remarkable lady, as you'll see. She was a part-time psychology student. We lived in flats around Auckland and both worked. And sat round in coffee bars being intellectuals. At one stage we lived in a converted lifeboat moored to the sewer-line in Hobson's Bay and spent our last ten bob on incense and guitar-strings.

I'd been turning aside from the impulse to write a book about deer-culling. It was the end of an era. The hunting now was being done by jetboat and helicopter. Deer farms were appearing everywhere. The old culler was obsolete. The back-country was falling into different hands. They even got cabbages and beef sent into the bush for them these days. Frame packs, down sleeping-bags, high-powered semi automatic rifles with telescopic sights, thermal underwear . . . . Pansies!

We were living under the name of Mr and Mrs Havisham (out of Dickens) in a flat in Park Road. Jean was working at a printery and I was writing my book. I called it *A Good Keen Man*. It took me about a month and I was just finishing typing it when two policemen came to interview me about lending my name to a bloke for a car deal he'd lashed on. I was already regarded with deep suspicion by our landlady – there was a part in my book where one of the characters gets the end of the toilet-roll caught in his dressing-gown belt and comes out through a hospital ward with it trailing out behind him. I wanted to see if this would actually work so I went along the hall to the toilet and pulled the toilet paper out the door and round the corner. I was partway up the passage when the landlady came in the front door with a bag of groceries.

"Mr Havisham!" she called out. "What on earth do you think you're doing with the toilet paper?"

"It's just something I'm writing," I stammered.

"I don't allow writing on the toilet paper, Mr Havisham," she barked. "This is a respectable house, I'll have you know. I'll just thank you to roll it up again and leave it as it was."

Anyone who's tried to roll up a length of toilet-paper again will tell you that it's just about impossible to leave it the way it was.

Anyway the visit from the policemen was the final straw. She gave us a week's notice for "bringing the police around the place. This is a respectable house, I'll have you know, Mr Havisham!"

I just had time to finish off my book.

I offered it to a publisher, who returned it saying that its publication would be profitable neither to them or me. I offered it to another publisher who wouldn't read it. I sent it to Reeds in Wellington, who wrote back to say they'd like to publish it, if I agreed to go through it with a journalist to knock it into shape. Okay, I said, or words to that effect.

We set off for Wellington in a 1934 Chev car we bought for fifteen quid, and it took us three months to get there. Had a fair bit of trouble with that car. We camped in the usual one-room flat and gave our right name because of the book. I got a job driving trucks and earthmoving machinery on the new Wellington airport. Jean worked as a waitress. In the evenings and on weekends Alex and I worked on THE BOOK. He taught me a lot about putting one together. More to it than I'd thought.

Jean was a good friend of James Baxter the poet and his wife Jackie. Jimmy and I hit it off pretty well and we had quite a few good times together. Jim was one of the most ardent people I ever met. He was even ardent about delivering the mail when he was a postman. He was an ardent alcoholic when I first met him, then he went on to be an ardent Roman Catholic, an ardent crusader and then an ardent recluse. A great bloke, Jim.

After a few months the book was finished. Ready for publication! They paid me fifty pounds advance royalties, which we put down as a deposit on an old V8 ute and took off to a rabbitting job at Pongoroa in the Wairarapa. We'd been there for a while when copies of the new book arrived. I'd written a book and had it published and been paid fifty quid for it. There might even be more money in it yet. That, as far as I was concerned, was all there was to that particular adventure.

I enjoyed rabbitting. You walk through the countryside with a shotgun and a pack of dogs, I used about sixteen of them. The dogs flushed out the rabbits and you shot them, or the dogs caught them, or they got into a burrow, in which case you threw in a handful of Cyanogas and filled in the entrance. It was good work, and it wasn't impossible to slip in a bit of pig-hunting or deerstalking when you got bored with rabbits.

Jean and I were just settling into a routine when all hell broke loose. *A Good Keen Man* was a runaway success, already into its fourth printing in a few months. Wads of newspaper-cuttings saying extravagant things about my writing. A cheque for hundreds of pounds. One journalist wrote that he doubted Crump's ability to produce such prose, the stuff was obviously ghost-written. I wanted to go and find him and rip his head off. I was already getting affected by it.

Would I be interested in writing another book? I wrote it in about three weeks and called it *Hang on a Minute Mate*. It was my first venture into proper fiction and I was more apprehensive about it than I had been about my first book. The publishers said they liked it so I could only wait and see.

We moved to Taupo, where each rabbitter used a hundred shotgun cartridges a day. Rabbits everywhere! After a couple of months we moved to a rabbitting job at Reporoa, where it was quieter. Then *Hang on a Minute Mate* came out and was an instant success. I was into fiction, and I liked the idea. I was a writer. Good fun!

With the money we were getting from book royalties we could afford a better set of wheels, so we got some. An old station wagon with a radio in it. And having got the wheels we had to use them, naturally. We wound up living in a flat near a beach out of Christchurch, where I wrote another book. Then we bought a big old wartime Morris gun-tractor off a mate of ours at Ngahere and took off down the West Coast, hunting venison for a shilling a pound.

For a year we lived in huts and in the gun-tractor and shot deer handy to the road. We borrowed horses and packed meat out of the Mahitahi and Paringa valleys. We got a system going where I shot deer up in the bush, head-shooting them with a .22 to cut down on noise, and dragged them down to the riverbed and hung them up for Jean to carry out to the road. In the whitebait season we ran a trench on the Paringa and made a few quid that way.

A year of that was enough for both of us. We moved to Wellington where we rented a bed-sitter and had a spell in town. Jean liked the city, just to walk around in, she reckoned. We did a lot of walking the streets at night, talking, but I can't for the life of me remember anything we talked about. I got to quite like the sights and sounds and smells of a sleeping city. It's got an atmosphere of its own.

During this time a bunch of the shooters from the fifties organised the first Deer-Cullers' Reunion, in the Korere Valley Pub out of Nelson. There were about ten of us and it was a hard case do. None of us could sing but that didn't stop anyone, and our efforts were hilarious. We drank the pub out of beer and had to send to Nelson for more kegs. It went on continuously for three days and nights. To me it was, in a way, the final hilarity.

There've been a few Deer-Cullers' Reunions since then, some of them quite big affairs, hundreds of people, but that first one in Korere Valley stands out in my memory as the last of the early years atmosphere. We were as fit and hard as you get, and yet we were like children, in those days before any of us knew anything about taking life seriously. Kind of free and totally at ease with one another. Fighting was almost unheard of and unthought of among us, we'd been through too much hard going together for that, but we argued and shouted and ganged up on each other according to the occasion and shoved each other around like schoolboys do.

Any policeman observing our behaviour would have been justified in refusing any of us a permit to own a firearm (and yet I never heard of a shooting accident among the professional hunters). The men who replaced us in the back country were required to be more responsible and conscious of the environment than we were. Out of date at twenty-two!

Jean and I split up. I didn't think we'd ever team up again. Then I met and married Fleur, a poet, an academic and librarian. She worked at the Alexander Turnbull Library. It was a turbulent affair, we went through the whole relationship in about five months. Then she went off to run the Colonial Office Library in London and I went off to find Jean and apologise for being an idiot. She thoroughly agreed with me. Just as well Fleur and I didn't have any children.

My third book, *There and Back*, had been a success. It was also given the Hubert Church Award for Prose. We bought a Land Rover and shipped it to Australia. I was working on another book and Jean flew to Sydney before me. I'll never forget seeing her off at the Wellington airport. Green pants, brown jersey, red scarf. Her only luggage was a flax kit with some books and stuff in it (not even full), and her money and papers in a copper teapot she'd found in a second-hand shop in Molesworth Street.

The reason why I couldn't go to Australia at the same time as Jean was because when I went to get a birth certificate for my passport they said at the Papatoetoe post office that no one of my name had ever been registered there. There were hassles and delays as they checked and re-checked. No such person as Barry John Crump. It took weeks to find out what the story was, I'd been registered as John Barrie Crump. There was no such person as Barry Crump.

This was a turn-up. Johnny Crump, eh! I wouldn't have minded, never liked the name Barry anyway, but the hassles involved in changing my name at this stage were too much to even think about, I decided to continue sailing under false colours. They let me put my usual name on my passport and I left for Australia about ten days after Jean did.

By the time I arrived in Sydney Jean had our Land Rover organised and a flat jacked up, where I finished off the book. She got a job at the place where my books were being printed, Halstead Press, which was a bit lucky for them because it was Jean who noticed that a run of my first two books they were doing were mixed up. They had half of one book and half the other bound together. They guillotined them apart, shuffled them into sequence and bound it all together under the title *Two in One*.

Printing was a much more cumbersome and expensive thing than it is today. Each letter was made of lead and had to be poured into a mould. Alteration was costly and done unwillingly, and if they wanted to re-print anything they had to pay for the hire and storage of the lead. An impressive amount of lead went into the making of a book.

The one I was writing was done. I sent it off to the publishers, and then we drove off through the centre of Australia towards the Gulf of Carpentaria. I'd grown a bit weary of sneaking up on animals and blowing them away with a rifle. I'd heard that the big saltwater crocodile in northern Australia was a different proposition altogether. I was going to have a go at him.

But not yet. We had to get there first. It's hard for us Kiwis to comprehend the vast size of Australia. It's nothing out of the ordinary to run into people who travel the length of New Zealand to do their shopping. After a few adventures and diversions, like a couple of weeks opal-digging at Lightning Ridge and a few days at a roo-shooters' camp, we arrived at Burketown on the Gulf of Carpentaria. We were in croc country. Great place, the north of Aussie, with its incredible variety of birds and other wildlife, its climate and its freedom. I wouldn't have ever left there except for fate.

Enquiries at the Burketown pub left us in no doubt that Harry Blue was the best croc-shooter in the area. He was away at some lagoons or other but due back any time, so we camped by the Leichardt River and waited for him. He came after a few days. A Latvian, solitary sort of bloke but friendly enough. He didn't mind showing us how to shoot crocs, and a few days later we loaded up with supplies and followed Harry's old Blitz truck off around the coast.

After two days' travel, mostly off any kind of road, we came to a big river with paperbark trees along each bank, where we camped. I'd come a long way for this and I was keen to get stuck into these here crocodiles, but Harry decided not to go out that night. Too much moon. The following night was cloudy and we pushed off an hour or so after dark, Harry paddling in the front of his little plywood dinghy with a spotlight on his forehead.

As a young boy (centre) with brother Colin (left) and Bill.

Ruatahuna Base Camp.

We tripped up and down the Barrier Reef – plenty of adventures.
All sorts of unusual wildlife.

He taught me how to use a shotgun . . .

We lived at Cooktown for a year – croc-shooting up the rivers.

At Te Teko I assembled a pack of dogs and got back into hunting . . .

He's a hard case piece of work the crocodile.

One of the little blokes. They can still do some damage.

Eighteen pointers were common in those days, though I myself never shot a decent head. We were more after numbers!

When a spotlight hits a crocodile's eyes they light up bright red. You paddle quietly up to him and shoot him through the head at point-blank range and get him into the boat before he sinks. That's what you do with the Johnson Freshwater crocodile. They're not considered dangerous to people, they only grow to an average of six to eight feet (though Harry and I got an eleven-footer at a lagoon once). The big Saltwater crocodile is quite a different story.

We got forty-five croc-skins in ten days or so and returned to Burketown with them. I hadn't seen anything I couldn't handle yet, but I knew there was more coming up.

Harry liked having Jean and me around. We were real bush-men, he reckoned. On our next trip we went to another river further round the Gulf, and Harry got out the big-croc gear. A twelve-foot harpoon-pole with a nine-inch iron quill, double barbed, fitted into the end of the pole, with an eighty-foot nylon rope attached to it. You stabbed the quill into the croc's neck and pulled the pole off it. Then you waited with the .303 ready for him to come to the surface. You might have to wait for half an hour or more for him to come up the first time, and that's a hell of long time to sit there waiting. As soon as you see his eyes in the light you start smacking him in the side of the head with the .303. You'd have to be lucky to get him the first time. He'll go down again but it might only be ten or fifteen minutes before he comes up this time. You start shooting again. Suddenly one of your bullets pen-etrates the thick rubbery skull and the croc rolls half sideways in the water. You paddle across and loop the rope round and round its jaws. Then you chop him through the spine at the back of the head with the axe to make absolutely sure. Then you float him to the shore and tie him there to be skinned next day. At that range a .303 will go through an axe-head, but it won't go through a wet blanket hanging up or a big crocodile's head.

He's a hard-case piece of work, the crocodile. He hasn't altered in three hundred million years, they reckon. You'd never tame one, there's something prehistoric about them. You have to make sure you do everything right when you go after him. One flick from that tail and you're history. He doesn't run away from you because he doesn't know anything about being attacked.

The first time I saw that big horny head and ridged snout lying in the water with our little boat drifting in on it I got real nervous. There's a knack in pushing yourself away as you drive the harpoon into him. Harry was careful to show me that, and I was careful to get it right, practicing on floating logs.

We got nine salties on that trip, the biggest was twelve feet long but Harry wasn't impressed. We hadn't seen a really big bloke yet. We'd got quite a few freshies as well and at a pound an inch, measured across the widest part of the belly, the money was good.

He was a hard man, Harry. While I'd been milking cows and shooting deer, he'd been fighting in the war. He had some pretty horrific yarns and ideas and scars on him from his experiences. He'd been hunting crocs in Northern Australia for about ten years almost entirely on his own, and he'd developed his own methods of getting them.

He told me that when people wanted to go croc-hunting with him he usually took them to the hardest place around, maybe deep in some tidal mangrove swamp where the clouds of mosquitos are so thick it's hard to see through them and any bare skin is either black with mossies or stinging with insect-repellent, day or night, except that in the daytime you've got hordes of vicious little sandflies that can go through a mosquito-net as well. It can get highly inhospitable in some of those places.

"They mostly go back to town again," said Harry.

I understood him perfectly. If you can't handle the worst of it you shouldn't be there at all.

"Why didn't you do that to us?" I asked him.

"You didn't come from the town,' he said. "Your wife is even a bushman."

We were flattered.

Jean had an imperturbable contentedness about her. She was happy whatever we were doing, and some of the work was hard. After a good night's hunting we could have ten or a dozen crocs to skin and scrape and pack in salt. They're tougher to skin than a big stag's neck in the roar and harder still to scrape the meat and fat off, even small ones, and Jean scraped her share of them.

Most days we'd finish the skins and flop in the shade and sleep the rest of the afternoon under mosquito nets. In the evening we'd wake and eat and paddle off in our little boat, raking the river with our light for the red blaze of crocodiles' eyes. And Jean pulled her weight with everything we did. Good value to have around.

It was finer, closer hunting than any I'd done before. You have to glide right up to the croc completely silent, with your light in his eyes so he can't tell how close you are. The slightest sound can put him down. Then you're right on top of him and everything has to be done exactly right, the harpoon quill must go in beside the thick shield at the back of its neck. Your bullet must hit him flat in the side of the head or you'll only give him a fright, if crocodiles get frights, Harry wasn't sure.

Quilling a crocodile with your harpoon was only the first thing, Harry reckoned. He's not yours until you've been paid for his skin. He'd lost three months' skins one year because of scale-slip. Not enough salt on them.

We did quite a few croc-shooting trips with Harry and got some good crocs and skins, but nothing really big. Harry kept telling me I'd run into 'One of the Big Blokes' one of these days. And he'd grin.

Harry had this dog, a white Alsatian. I've never liked Alsatian dogs, they go weak in the hips, they're no good for hunting and they tend to intimidate people. Another thing this dog of Harry's had against him was that Alsatian dogs were illegal in Queensland and the Northern Territory, because if they get away they're liable to breed with the dingoes and the pups are the best sheep-worriers ever known. It was a risk to be seen with an Alsatian dog up there. If you saw one you could walk up and shoot it with impunity.

But regardless of all that, Harry's dog was one of the best I ever knew. He understood the scene. He and I got a crocodile in the moonlight on a dried-up lagoon. A seven-foot freshy, the dog bailed it and I clobbered it with a didgeridoo I was sneaking off to practise. I carted it back and dumped it by the fire and told Jean to stick a bullet through its head in case it wasn't properly dead yet. Even Harry was impressed by that. I can bung on an act when I want to.

He was a great-value dog. When we swam, he swam outside us. When we walked he walked in front and indicated everything we mightn't have noticed. He told Jean the King Brown snake was in the mosquito net. He – he was one of the best dogs I ever knew, and it's how he died that I want to tell you about.

Harry wanted to spend the wet season up a river in Arnhem Land. Heaps of crocs and plenty of salt on the big salt-pans to pack the skins in. Jean and I didn't want to commit ourselves to three months in one place, so we agreed to give him a hand to get his gear there and then we'd go across to Cairns and wait out the wet there.

Harry's equipment is worth describing. Ropy's grandmother chose a sapling for his canoe, and eighty years or so later Ropy went there and chipped his way through the tree and spent weeks making a fourteen-foot canoe out of it. Then he paddled and pulled and sailed and poled it a hundred miles to Borroloola, where Harry bought it off him for two bags of flour, some sugar, some plugs of niki-niki tobacco, a few feet of wire and a packet of Kelloggs Cornflakes. That was Harry's small canoe. He had a larger one about twenty feet long. I don't know how he obtained that one.

He had two rifles, a .303 and a .22, some spears and a harpoon, ropes, an axe, knives and a coil of number-eight wire for fish-spearheads and trading. A tarpaulin was his only shelter. We dipped his bags of flour in the water and left them in the sun so a hard waterproof layer would form on the inside of the bags. His rice and matches and carbide for his light and sugar, tea and other food was all packed into tins.

He had two aborigine skinners going with him, Duke and Peta, a hard-case looking pair. I was going to help them get the canoes of gear there and meet Jean with the Land Rover at a station on the Roper River where friends of ours were staying. It was only a hundred miles or so across country, but the way we had to go it was twice that far.

By the time Harry and I and our two skinners and Harry's dog set off we were starting to worry about the wet season coming in early and cutting us off. There were storms on the horizon already. We made it down to the coast the first day and camped there, and from then on things started going wrong.

We found it was easier to pull the canoes along in the shallow water at the edge of the beach than to paddle them out in the sea side-on to the waves. The second day we made about thirty wearying miles around the coast, Harry and I pulling the small canoe and Duke and Peta following with the bigger one. We'd just decided to look for somewhere to camp for the night when Peta broke his paddle trying to lever the canoe off a sandbar.

This was a bit of a disaster. A good aborigine paddle is a work of art. Six feet long, carved from a single piece of wood, shaped to fit the hand and so beautifully tapered in the blade that it doesn't dribble when you lift it out of the water properly, important when you're gliding up to a crocodile. And Peta had broken his one. While we set up a camp he went off along the coast to find a log for a new paddle. He returned after a couple of hours and dumped an eight-foot log, had a feed of rice and stingray and went off again, back the way we'd come from. He brought another log back during the night and in the morning he'd started chipping a paddle out of the first log with a sheath-knife.

Along the horizon we could see the black clouds gathering and hear thunder like distant gunfire, but Peta wasn't shifting until his paddle was finished. He chipped away all day and into the night. By the next morning the paddle was taking shape. He was using the hard sole of his bare foot to prevent the knife from chopping too deeply into the surface of the wood. We could feel the storms by this time, and see the lightning-flashes out to sea. By that night Peta was scraping a finish on his paddle with broken glass from a bottle we'd found washed up.

It cost us two days, that paddle, and although it was a real good one (I ended up with it and used it for years) it wasn't worth the trouble the delay caused. As we made our way round the coast it started to look as though the wet was going to hit us before we could reach the Roper, and Duke and Peta were getting slower and sulkier with every mile, demanding tobacco, deliberately dropping behind so we'd eventually have to go back and urge them along. Things like that.

Crossing the Limmin rivermouth was a hassle we didn't need. The land is so flat here that a wind blowing in from the Gulf can hold the full tide up-river for three or four tides, and the river-mouths are often turbulent and tricky to negotiate. Both our canoes got swept out in a wide arc into the sea and it was a long paddle back round to the beach. Everything was wet so we lit two big fires and rested up for the rest of that day. It would have been difficult to get Duke and Peta moving again anyway.

The next morning I went across to help Duke and Peta shove the big canoe into the water and Duke said, "Me go walkabout now boss," and he started walking towards the scrub-line at the top of the beach. I called out to Harry that this bloke was going walkabout.

We hadn't been using the rifles, we had one in each canoe wrapped up against the salt water, which turned out to be dead lucky for Duke. Harry took one look at him and grabbed a kangaroo-spear and woomera out of the small canoe. Duke saw him and started running. Harry let strip with the spear and it went right through Duke's leg. He went down among some driftwood at the high-water line, yelling his head off. Harry grabbed another spear and poised it at Peta, who hadn't moved. You could see he wasn't going to. I ran up to Duke. The head of the spear had gone right through the calf of his leg.

"You've hit him!" I called out to Harry. "Bring something to cut this spear off with."

Harry came up and handed me a knife. He was holding the spear for stabbing.

"Pull it out if you like," he said, "But we have to kill him anyway."

"What the hell do you mean, kill him?" I said.

"We have to. If he gets back to his tribe and tells them we speared him, his whole family will look for us, and if they find us they tie us to a tree and cut out our kidney and sit in front of us and eat it. Then they leave us for the ants."

"What the hell do you mean by *us*?" I said. "I haven't done anything to him."

"Us," said Harry. "We have to kill him."

"Like hell," I said. "You're not killing anyone while I'm around. What did you go and spear him for, anyway. He's no good to us like this."

"If he'd got away Peta would have followed him and we would have been stranded here. This way we have one of them. Peta won't go walkabout on his own now."

"Well you're not killing Duke, and that's that," I told him.

I should have known from Harry's stories about the things he had to do in the war that he didn't regard human life as precious as some of us, but being this close to it was a bit horrifying.

Harry looked at Duke expressionless for a moment or two and then shrugged and went back down to the canoes. I got Peta to hold the spear steady while I chewed through it with the knife behind Duke's leg and drew it out the front. Peta was so nervous he was almost spastic. I thought Duke was being pretty stoical about it all because he didn't cry out or anything, but he'd fainted. There wasn't much bleeding and it seemed to have slid in beside the bone, but it was still a hell of a mess.

That spear-head had been cut out of a forty-four gallon drum and bound onto the shaft with a bulb of twine and beeswax about an inch and a half thick. It had dragged quite a bit of meat out with it, and an abo's leg isn't all that thick. I bandaged him up with a strip of canvas and gave him water, and Peta and I carried him down and propped him up in the middle of the big canoe. Harry ignored him. Peta and I pulled the big canoe with Duke in it and Harry led the way dragging the small canoe on his own, and he was hard to keep up with.

By the time we reached the Roper Rivermouth there were storms and rain lashing across the coast every few hours. At the Roper we needed to cross to the far side, and with the tide running out and the wind blowing in there was quite a rip and chop. I didn't trust Harry alone with Duke, didn't like the way he looked at him, and Peta and I paddled across with Duke first and made it okay. But Harry caught a squall and over-turned in the small canoe only twenty yards from us.

We recovered everything that floated, most of it was in tins, but the .303 had gone into the drink. Harry needed that rifle if he was to survive the wet.

"I'll dive for it," he said.

We knew exactly where he'd turned over and he swam out and began diving. It was about twelve feet deep and the water was muddy. On about his fourth dive Peta gave a shout. The head of a big crocodile had surfaced right near where Harry was diving. It sank out of sight as he came up for air.

"Get out of there!" I shouted. "There's a big croc near you!"

"I touched the rifle that time," he called back, and then he dived again.

After a hell of a long time the canvas-wrapped barrel of the rifle broke the surface of the water and Harry swam to the bank. I dragged him out onto dry land. This adventure was get-ting almost too adventurous.

We sorted out the gear, we fortunately hadn't lost much, and then paddled upstream for a mile or so and set up camp on the riverbank and lit a big fire. We'd been there for about an hour when Harry's dog, who usually patrolled the perimeter of a new camp for snakes and things, suddenly started screaming down by the edge of the river. We ran over there and saw a big crocodile with a white nose swimming away with Harry's dog in its jaws, dunking him under the water and then bringing him out and crushing him then dunking him again. Then the dog was silent.

The croc swam across the river and climbed out on a sand bar and broke up the dog, tossing it around in its jaws. There was something arrogant about it. We had the .303 in bits drying it out. I was pinging away at the croc with the .22 until Harry pulled at my arm to give it up. The croc, a heavy set fifteen-footer, lunged off into muddy water with the broken bloody bundle that had been Harry's dog, and he was gone. It was the biggest crocodile I'd ever seen at that stage.

"Sorry about that, Harry," I said

He shrugged and turned away towards the camp. I knew how he felt. I'd had my share of good dogs killed.

We tried for that white-nosed crocodile that night with a spotlight and a harpoon but he wouldn't let us find him. (Years later a letter from Harry caught up with me to tell me he'd harpooned White-nose and avenged his dog.)

We had to keep moving up the river. The rains were literally right on top of us. Duke's leg was swollen and red and blue and peeling. He was obviously pretty crook. Harry seemed to have abandoned the idea of finishing him off, but I still kept an eye on them both in case Harry was trying to bluff me. It was a constant worry.

Two days upriver we finally drifted to the bank below the station buildings, and from the top of the bank I could see our Land Rover parked beside a building and Jean and another woman hanging out washing. I gave our whistle and Jean and I ran towards each other like people in some movie.

We told them at the station that Duke had been speared by

74

accident. They called up the Flying Doctor on their radio and as we loaded Duke into the plane you could see he wished Harry had speared him properly. He was terrified.

The bloke at the Doomidgee Mission told me later that the practice of eating the kidney of a feudal enemy had been long since discontinued, but then so was the practice of lobbing a kangaroo-spear through an abo's leg to stop him going walka-bout. I was wary of every strange abo I met after that, but I've still got both kidneys.

I traded Peta a knife and some rope for his paddle and he took Duke's one. A couple of days later Harry and Peta set off up-river to find some lagoons they knew of, and Jean and I scarpered across to Cairns, just ahead of the wet season all the way.

That was the last time we saw Harry. About a year later a prospector we met said he'd camped with him on the Nicholson River. Harry's croc-boat had come off the back of his truck somewhere between Seven Emus and Calvert Hills, about a hundred miles across-country, and he was hunting crocodiles using two Holden bonnets welded together for a boat. Incredibly unstable, but that was Harry. He survived all right. Brother Bill worked with him at The Isa many years later.

In Cairns we got a bloke to make us a proper paddling dinghy and assembled the rest of the gear for crocs and as soon as the wet was over off we went. Croc-shooters!

We got a few, too. About a thousand of them over the next couple of years. Two hundred-odd salties, including four or five Big Blokes. But I'll never be able to forget the first Big Bloke I ran across. We'd arrived at a branch of the Limmin River and camped there. Not far from the camp I came across some fresh pig-sign. We could use the meat so I went back and grabbed the .22 and a handful of bullets and started tracking the pigs upstream.

It was late summer and the river here had dried up into a series of long lagoons with dry riverbed in between. About a quarter of a mile from the camp I suddenly saw a huge crocodile in the riverbed up ahead, two hundred yards from the nearest water. And I tell you, he was a Big Bloke. Eighteen feet of him, bulging hugely out behind his four foot-long head. A ton and a half of him. It took me a few seconds to believe what I was looking at.

He'd heard me coming, and he was facing me with his mouth open, and I had a pea-rifle in my hand. I kept about thirty yards away from him and close to a leaning tree and emptied the magazine into his mouth. He didn't move, so I decided to have a go at shooting his eyes out. I got round the side of him and hit him in the eye with about the fourth shot. And he didn't like it. His tail thrashed around and flung sticks and rocks across the riverbed. Then he spewed up some bones and balls of wallaby-fur and half a small crocodile and some of the stones they eat to keep their buoyancy neutral.

I ran round and got his other eye with about the fifth shot. I knew I had blinded him because he blundered straight into the bank and began to feel his way clumsily down towards the water. I had to kill him now.

I left the .22 leaning against the bank and ran like hell across the mulga to our camp. Jean was coming towards the camp dragging firewood. I grabbed the .303 and a handful of ammo and yelled at her to follow me and hared it back upstream. When I got back the croc was making his way downstream towards a deep lagoon. He still had about sixty yards to go when I started shooting him in the head with the .303. It only took three shots to get one into his brain, and another three to make sure of him. I then sat on the ground with my head in my hands, shaking and weak, looking up every now and then to make sure it had really happened. It took us all that day and half the next to knife the skin off him and scrape it and pack it in salt.

I've harpooned a few Big Blokes since then but nothing that big, and nothing that I ever had to get so close to on land in the open in daylight. It's an experience I'd probably flag away these days.

New Zealand for mountains and rivers and Australia for birds and insects. And some of the birds are pretty hard case, like the black crows. We were about forty miles out of Calvert Hills when we met up with an old prospector in a wreck of a ute. He lived 'just down here' and wanted someone to help him get rid of some crows that were giving him a bad time. We followed his ute-dust down a sideroad and 'just down here' turned out to be about thirty miles.

He lived in a shack near a big blue hole in the ground that was so rich in copper that he only had to dig a bit out now and again and sell it. He'd found it years before. He had an old aborigine couple living there but he needed a fourth for the crows, which were ruining his garden, and his temper, by the way he cursed the black bastards of things.

They'd wait until he left the shack and then fly in and get stuck into his garden. What they didn't eat they'd pull to bits or dig up. And there was no way they'd let him get within range of them with his old double-barreled shotgun.

The trouble was that they could count, up to three, the old bloke reckoned. If three people went into the hut and only two came out and left, the crows wouldn't come near the place. They'd know there was still someone in the hut. So Jean and I and the old abo couple and the prospector all went into his cluttered little shack and had a brew of tea. Then Jean and I and the other couple left and got into their ute and drove away a few hundred yards. We'd just pulled up when BOOM! BOOM!

He'd got three of them and he was so gleeful about outwitting them we had to laugh. We outwitted them once more that evening and got two more. Next morning it was decided that the boss himself should leave with the others and I would wait behind and do the shooting, in case of super-crafty crows recognising him.

They took off in the ute and I watched through a crack in the doorway, and sure enough as soon as they were gone some crows flew in and sat in the branches of a gum tree above the garden. A couple of them dropped into the garden. When there were half a dozen of them I stepped outside and blew away two that were sitting together on a branch and got another as the rest flew away. The prospector was ecstatic.

The crows were keeping their distance. Later that day I picked one off with the .22 at about seventy yards, and then blew a shower of bark off a tree beside one with the .303 at about a hundred and fifty yards. That rocked them. It was the only time I ever noticed black crows to be silent, and none came near the garden for the rest of the time we were there.

The old bloke reckoned it might give him enough of a break to get his plants up. He had a row of dead crows hanging on his garden fence and he only had to fire a shot now and again to keep them away, until they sussed him out again. Jean put in a day helping him sort out his garden and I helped the old abo couple mine a few bags of copper-ore.

We'd been asked to drop off some supplies to an old Norwegian bloke who lived beside a river on the border between Queensland and the Northern Territory. He was wanted by the police in both states for various misdemeanors but if the Queensland police came to interview him he'd cross over to the Northern Territory side, and vice-versa.

He had a large collection of Aborigines living around him and no one could get near him without them knowing. His hut stank of burning camel-dung to try and keep the sandflies and mosquitos back a bit.

We camped there and Jean and I went out and got quite a big croc, twelve-footer, right near their camp. No one knew it was there and they reckoned we were pretty good croc shooters. We gave it to them to eat. Temporary heroes!

One of the abo blokes who'd helped us skin the croc, an old chap called Tarzan, invited me to come and harpoon a dugong down at the river-mouth.

"What's a dugong?" I asked the old Norwegian bloke.

"A sea-cow. They're quite big things. The blacks spear them out in the sea. They eat the meat and use the fat to keep the sandflies off themselves. Tastes a bit like beef."

Sounded okay to me, especially when I saw who was coming with Tarzan and me. An old lady called Rosie, about sixty. She carried a glowing gum-branch on a biscuit-tin lid, which she put in the dugout canoe we were going in. Some spears and ropes, mast and sail, butcher-knife stuck in a crack – all very simple. Jean was okay there, even though it looked as though we might be a bit late getting back with the dugong. Off we went, paddling down the river.

The river-mouth was a hell of a lot further away than I'd imagined. Hours further. It was getting dark by the time we reached the coast. We paddled straight out into the sea and kept going until we were out of sight of land. The coastal land is very low there and you don't have to be far out before you lose sight of it, but I was starting to wonder how far we were actually going to have to go to get one of these dugong. I was fit for paddling, I could paddle all day, but I wasn't so sure how long these two oldies were going to be able to keep it up, especially Rosie.

We'd been paddling for hours without a stop and I was starting to get a bit tired on it. I could paddle all day but I wasn't too sure about paddling all night as well. Rosie was still paddling along the same as when she started, only pausing to hold her gum-branch up in the wind to get it glowing again and light her pipe of niki-niki. Tarzan stood up in the prow every now and again to look around. There was half a moon and you could see quite a distance.

Tarzan got interested in something and stood up in the front with his harpoon-pole end-on to the breeze so it wouldn't warn the dugong. He'd heard something. Rosie dipped her pipe in the sea and we paddled on, changing direction wherever Tarzan pointed, which he did with his lips, because, as he told me later, the wind blows across your arm. Suddenly I heard something blow out to the side of us and Tarzan called for full steam ahead. I'd just about run out of steam by this time and as I put every effort I could into it I knew that if we had to do this again I wasn't going to be much use to us. I could hardly lift my paddle out of the water.

Tarzan's quill went straight into the dugong's shoulder. Then there was only the sound of the rope looping out over the front of the canoe. Tarzan back-paddled quickly to keep us straight-on and the canoe was suddenly snatched forward and dragged out to sea at a hell of a bat. These dugong were tough customers! I was thinking of the long paddle back to Australia.

Finally, I don't know how long, the dugong tired and we got it alongside the canoe. A big brown bristly fat body with a small flat head and spongy flippers. A good half-ton of it. Tarzan killed it behind the head. I couldn't imagine how we were going to get the thing into the canoe, but I had no imagination. It was simple; we just jumped out into the sea and sank the canoe and floated the dugong into it. Rosie holding the paddles and spears and her burning gum-branch on the biscuit-tin lid, me holding the mast and sail and harpoon and ropes, and Tarzan rocking the canoe to try and slop a bit of freeboard up.

Then other things turned up. You could see the streaks of phosphorous in the water as they dived in on the scent of dugong blood.

"What the hell's that in the water here!" I yelled at Tarzan.

"Sharks, boss," he said. "Little ones."

Those streaks in the water looked big enough to me. If something had touched me on the leg just then, tired as I was, I would have leapt screaming out of the water. And all this was happening about fifteen miles off the coast at night. We finally got enough water out of the canoe to start scooping it out in significant quantities with some big shells that were tied to the gunnel with string. I was very glad to get back into that boat again.

We could make use of a breeze that had come up going back so Tarzan fitted the mast and stuck the sail up. Rosie and pipe steered with her paddle in the stern and I dozed off leaning against the blubbery hide of the dugong in the middle of the canoe. It was getting daylight when we reached the river mouth. We surfed across the bar on a wave and were at last in the river again.

I imagined we might stop here for a spell, but no. The wind was no use to us any more so we paddled the overloaded canoe on up the river to the camp on a rising tide, arriving there about midday. By the time we got there I was as bushed as I'd ever been in my years of hunting. Those two old people had been paddling almost continuously for twenty-four hours without anything to eat or drink. To them it was a typical hunt, there's no way an ordinary bushman could keep up with that sort of thing. I was grateful to Tarzan and Rosie, they'd taught me to keep my mind open about who's good at paddling and who isn't.

The wet season was approaching so we shot through to Cairns and camped under a big mango tree on the outskirts of town.

People liked Jean, and she liked them. Wherever we went she made friends and, perhaps because we had so little, people were always giving her things, especially clothes. We were always trying to give away stuff she'd been given. In Cairns she made friends with a women whose husband was trying to sell a boat he had. He took us for a ride round the harbour in it. A twenty-seven-foot gaff-rigged scaled-down lugger with a two-cylinder, air-cooled Lister diesel in it. The *Waterwitch*. A tidy little boat.

We bought it off him for nearly all our croc-skin money, left our Land Rover with friends in Cairns, and took off up the coast with a chart spread out on the roof of the cabin.

CHAPTER FIVE

We were mad, neither of us had ever had anything to do with boats in our lives, and here we were blithely sailing off up the Great Barrier Reef, graveyard of ships. Several times we found ourselves among coral bombies and steered our way through them. We lost track of where we were on the chart and anchored for the night off a completely exposed beach. It just happened there was no wind that night.

Two days later we motored into the Endeavour River and tied up at the Cooktown wharf, blissfully unaware that we should have gone up on the reef at least four times on the way up from Cairns.

We lived at Cooktown for a year, camping in the boatshed on the old jetty, tripping up and down the Barrier Reef in our little boat, trailing off the headlands for Spanish mackerel, snorkeling on the reef, croc-shooting up the rivers, netting barramundi in the lagoons – plenty of adventures. There were three hundred-odd people living in Cooktown but hardly any of them had ever been out to the reef. We became the local experts.

It was within a hundred miles of Cooktown, paddling up the Daintry River with Jean and a tame pelican called Pelly that I saw the slide of the biggest crocodile I've ever seen the sign of. He'd been lying on sloping mud facing the river, and he'd lunged off into the water when we were probably still a quarter of a mile away. The slide of his belly was a foot deep in the thick tidal mud, and as wide as you can hold your arms apart. Its footprints, each one as big as the seat of a chair, were two full paces apart, over six feet. We paddled back downriver to where the *Waterwitch* was anchored. We weren't going to see anything more interesting than *that* up this river. It was a bit of a thrill to think something that big was somewhere under our dinghy in the muddy waters of the Daintry.

We heard later that the pilot of a light plane who was taking aerial photographs of the Great Barrier Reef spotted a huge crocodile on a sand-bar in the Daintry River. He returned and photographed it and it was estimated to be thirty feet long. It'd have to be the one Jean and I saw the sign of that day. He would have weighed two and a half to three tons; he would have been two to three hundred years old; he was a *Real* Big Bloke. How about that one, Harry!

That croc was subsequently protected by an act of the Queensland government, some years before all crocodiles were protected and the trade in their skins discontinued.

There were several reasons why I wasn't going to try and stick a harpoon into that one. I was good and scared of him, don't worry about that, but apart from that I didn't want to have killed a croc like him for the money for his skin, even if you could get it off him in one piece and move it around. It'd weigh something like a quarter of a ton and take two hundred pounds of salt to pack it in.

I'd have liked to find out what that croc had inside him though. He was quite capable of floating up alongside a drinking horse or cattle-beast and dragging it into the river. I've seen where a croc less than half his length and a quarter of his weight had snatched a half-grown pig as it trotted along the river bank, and burst its guts all over the bushes. This bloke could bust up any-sized pig, a kangaroo, a calf, a person — and swallow them on the spot.

We'd found some hard-case things inside crocodiles, especially the bigger salties. Things like a cattle ear-tag with WESTMOORLAND 14 on it, the brass plate off a dog collar, the leather eaten away from the rivets, a ball of nylon mesh where the croc had twisted a barramundi out of someone's fishing net, a shark hook caught in the corner of a fifteen-footer's mouth with a frayed length of quarter-inch wire rope trailing from it, an aluminium saucepan, the buckle off a belt ... and yet one of the biggest crocodiles I ever got, a massive, double-chinned sixteen-footer, was living on catfish and mud-crabs at the mouth of the Starkie River. He was easy.

I had to fly back to New Zealand to negotiate a contract or something and got held up there for a bit, so I wrote a book based on our croc-hunting adventures, in five days and nights, sitting in an armchair in Guy Powell's flat in Kelburn, in long-hand, in exercise books, and gave it to a public typist who claimed she could read my handwriting. I didn't see the book again until after it was published. *Gulf,* I called it. It was later reprinted under the new title *Crocodile Country.*

I ran into my Brother Bill the night before I was leaving to go back to Queensland and we yarned into the night about what it was like up there. As I was leaving next morning he suddenly said "Hang on till I get me boots, Brother Barry," and he got on the plane and came with me. Sent a telegram to his boss from Brisbane saying he wouldn't be back for a while. Bill fell for Australia straight away and spent many years there.

We fished and hunted up and down the Cape York Peninsula for many happy months, living on the jetty and the boat. A humming-bird started building its nest on the cord of our mosquito net. It was quite fascinating to watch it hover there and build up the nest and line it. Then it laid two tiny eggs in it.

We decided to do a croc-hunt up the Starkie River and when it came time to pull the mosquito net down Jean wouldn't hear of it. We left it behind and suffered the mosquitos in the swamps of the Starkie for nearly a week. Almost eaten alive because of a tiny humming-bird. Its chicks were so small we could put both of them in a teaspoon.

Cooktown was the first Australian town I'd really got to know, and what a crazy wonderful frontier-type place it was in those days. Two hundred miles from the nearest other town, Cairns, over a road that was frequently closed in the dry season and always closed in the wet. Most of the freight and passengers came and went on the *Malanda*, a hundred-foot boat that called in every two or three weeks. The population was mostly made up of people from all over who'd called in for the weekend and couldn't get away from the place, and they were as colourful as the place itself, the climate and the coast, the river and the reef, the history and the wildlife and the sheer abundance that was Cooktown in the fifties and sixties.

There was Rum Jungle Jim McKenzie; accidentally blew one of his trocus-shell divers' brains out with a rusty .44 rifle trying to scare away sharks when he was skippering a pearling-lugger in the Timor Sea, and he'd pensioned himself off in Cooktown, energetically blotting out the memory of floating brains and streaming blood with large shots of schnapps and beer chasers in Jimmy Adamson's pub, recounting experiences around the coasts and islands of north Australia that made me feel I was born too late for real adventure, dropping it on me for the loan of a quid until pension day before staggering off into the dark, still chuckling at his own last joke, to be beaten up by a wallaby he surprised in the porch of his shack down by the river.

Crazy Fomenco, towed back from trying to paddle to New Guinea in a ridiculous cockleshell of a boat, and now living in the mangrove swamps and plains up the coast from Cooktown, skinny as a wallaby-jack, eating mud-crabs and stolen sheep, dressed in skins and sleeping in the sand. He was sighted every so often, but he always took off as though the hounds of Hell were on his hammer, and no one had been able to catch him to tell him he wasn't being chased.

Then there was Quiet Eddie from Bundaberg, fishing out of Cooktown with Big Andy the bully, who arrived down at the wharf mad on rum and threatening to get Hungry Hogan (his triggerless .45 sixgun) and shoot Quiet Eddie for forgetting the bread. Eddie got into a bit of a panic and grabbed a .303 out of the dinghy and blew one through the leg of Big Andy, who went down on a bollard and put a rib through one of his lungs. No one noticed the hole through his thigh, all they could see was the blood round his mouth and thought he was at least lung-shot. They took him up to the hospital on the back of Jack Stewart's old green International truck. Eddie thought he'd killed a bloke and went along and gave himself up to the sergeant, who told him that if Big Andy lived he was going to arrest Eddie and charge him with failing to stamp out a public nuisance when he had the chance.

A week or two later, coming back down the coast from Thursday Island, we ran into Quiet Eddie and Big Andy fishing out on the reef with their freezer nearly full of Spanish Mackerel and coral-trout. Great mates!

And the Good Father from the Parish up the hill, rosy-nosed from early morning prayer, shuffling at six in the morning into the Sovereign Hotel, where Bert was usually cleaning up with a glass of over-proof rum stashed under the bar, to ask if he might have a 'wee pint for me sciatica' and reaching over when Bert's back was turned to top up his handle from the wrong tap and gulp down half a pint of the Epsom salts Bert was cleaning out the beer-pipe with.

The valiant Father latched himself into the hotel lavatory and, refusing all offers of help and protesting that he was perfectly all right, he fought it out alone with the evil forces within until the afternoon.

And The Arab, standing there with a ten-foot rock-python called Arthur affectionately entwined around his bare shoulders and leg, his face ashine with sincerity as he entreated me to bring him any Taipan or Death-adder snakes I ran across. The Arab used to claim that the Taipan was the most misunderstood of all the snakes. All we understood about them was that the venom in one bite from one of them could kill two hundred sheep. All we ever wore when we were out in the mulga was a pair of shorts, and Jean kept a bikini-top handy for scraping croc-skins or if we ran into anyone unexpectedly. We were vulnerable to snakes and didn't share The Arab's rapport with them. We gave them a wide berth.

Then there was Billy Tea, Harbourmaster. Lived in a cottage down by the rivermouth and it was his job to polish the reflectors and fill with kerosene the two lights that guided boats in over the bar and into the Endeavour River. Billy went on a binge every so often to douse his chronic ulcers in gallons of beer, in case they went away and left him with nothing to worry about. Sometimes it would take him a week or more to get crook enough to have to stop, and the lights would fade down, the reflectors would blacken, one would go out altogether – which one? We cursed our good friend Billy Tea as we eased the *Waterwitch* across the bar by instinct, guesswork and good luck.

Billy held a Skipper's Ticket but he hadn't been to sea since his forty-foot tugboat got caught by Cyclone Bella in fifty-six. He was heading into Port Douglas when the storm hit him and rolled the tug over. Billy was knocked out and when he came round the boat was lying on its side two hundred yards inland from high water. He lost all faith in a life on the briny after that, and he wouldn't even row out to service his lights without first carefully checking on the weather. A squall on the horizon in the morning could cause him to abandon the job for the whole day if his ulcers were playing up on him.

In spite of his determination to remain unnecessarily numbered among the afflicted, Billy Tea was one of the nicest blokes you could ever meet, and it was impossible to stay hacked off with him for long.

Old Peter the remittance man was a hard shot. He lived under some canvas under a big tree outside of town. He always wore a filthy blue pinstriped suit with the crutch split nearly right round, and, thus attired, he walked into town every day to tell everyone he met that he'd seen it snow in Sydney in nineteen thirty-nine. He hadn't found anyone who believed him yet, but he never gave up. It might be interesting to look up the weather records for that year.

Peter wasn't exactly famous for his attention to personal hygiene, and to stand anywhere near him rendered one uncomfortably aware of the reason for the stitching in his strides having given out on him. He always seemed to have shaved with a breadknife or something, and the toenails sticking out through the split in the front of his shoe were long overdue for attention from a farrier. It was strange to hear such cultured English accents spoken by such a poor decrepit wreck of a bloke. The locals looked after old Peter as best they could and made sure he got a feed under his belt every now and then.

Jack, the Cooktown hardware man and undertaker, was high up in the Buffalo Lodge, and he put it on me to join them because a real high Buffalo from the Grand Lodge Of England was coming on a visit to personally 'Elevate' some of the local

Buffs, including Jack, and he was very embarrassed. They didn't have enough members to fill the offices. Would I come to the rescue?

"Okay, Jack, what do I have to do?"

I had to be initiated. It was a hard-case affair with speeches and rituals, and I came out of there a Member of the Royal Antediluvian Order of Buffaloes, Cook-161, holding the office of Treasurer, a notebook, a bag of money and two badges, one for membership and the other for service as an officer of the Lodge.

That part of it was okay, but from the time I went to the second meeting things started going wrong. Due to the shortage of Buffs in this part of the world they'd recruited old Frank the Abo and elected him to guard the door and make sure that only genuine Buffaloes could get in. Now Frank wasn't bad at skinning crocs or scratching tin or straightening a kangaroo-spear, but he wasn't exactly what you'd call good officer-material. For one thing he took the job too seriously.

We'd been out on the reef and I was a few minutes late getting to the meeting. I knocked on the door and a slide in it opened and Frank looked out. All I could see of him was his eyes and his teeth and the blade of the sword held up by his ear at attention.

"G'day, Frank," I said. "Sorry I'm a bit late."

"Password!" he said.

I'd been told the password for getting into the Lodge meetings, but I couldn't remember it. It was a bit of a complicated thing that didn't make sense.

"Sorry, Frank. What is it again? I've just forgotten it."

"Password!"

"Come on, Frank. You know I'm a member. You were there when they initiated me. Let me in."

"Password!"

"Damn it Frank, I'm the bloody treasurer. I've just forgotten the password, that's all."

"You don't get in unless I get the secret password," said Frank, and he closed the slide.

I was half-thinking of going back to the boat when one of the other members arrived and knocked on the door. The slide slid open.

"Password!"

He gave the password, the door opened and he went in and the door closed again, but I'd heard enough of it to remember. I knocked on the door, the slide slid open.

"Password!"

I gave the password, the door opened and Frank stood with his sword-hand yellow-knuckled at attention as I entered. I gave him a dirty look that completely failed to penetrate the authority of his position as Keeper of the Tile.

Our next meeting was when the Worthy Primo from the Grand Lodge of England would be here, and the correct procedures had to be rehearsed, the jewels polished and the hall decorated. And what a spectacle it was in the rusty corrugated-iron shed beside the mangrove inlet on the Endeavour River, within yards of where Captain Cook's men first set foot in Australia, almost two hundred years before.

The Grand bloke from England had three other blokes with him, all high up in the Lodge, judging by their regalia. They wore sashes and aprons, chains and medals and badges and braid and embroidery. Beside them we all looked drab and grubby. Frank demanded the password from the Grand Bloke and his entourage, and got it and an approving pat on the arm from the King Buff Himself, which still failed to shake Frank's rigid attention to duty.

We were all seated according to rank and the proceedings kicked off with the business of an ordinary meeting, the ceremonies would come later. We hurried through the agenda until they asked for the treasurer's report.

I stood up and explained how I hadn't actually got around to doing any treasuring yet, I'd had to use the money for something else, but as soon as the cheque for some croc skins came through I was going to bank the Lodge money and pay the accounts. Then I sat down again.

I thought they were going to leave it at that, but then The Worthy Primo from the Grand Lodge of England stuck his oar in.

"This is highly irregular," he said. "I'm not sure that I've ever heard of this kind of thing taking place in the Lodge."

"Er – well, yes," stammered Jack. "We'll obviously have to sort out our finances at our next meeting."

That should have taken care of the matter, but the Grand Bloke's mates had to get in on the act.

"Most irregular," said one of them pursing his lips seriously.

"It's a criminal offence, misappropriating funds, isn't it?" suggested another.

"It'll certainly have to be fully investigated," announced someone else.

"I think we're at least entitled to some sort of explanation," the Grand Bloke said to me. "Have you got anything to say about your offhand attitude towards the Lodge funds?"

I stood and told them how I'd only been the treasurer for one meeting and didn't think it made any difference what money I banked or when I banked it. I wasn't trying to rip anyone off and couldn't see what they were going on about.

It took them half an hour to decide to remove me from office until the matter could be resolved. I was in disgrace at my third meeting of the Royal Antediluvian Order of Buffloes. The meeting never did come completely right after that. There was a shadow hanging over it – me. Jack got elevated to higher rank, though, and could wear more jewels and chains.

My cheque came through and I banked the Buff-money and wrote up the notebook, but my fellow-Buffs had lost all confidence in my financial abilities. They gave the job to Frank and put me on the door.

Bob, the policeman at Cooktown, is worth a mention. Six feet of him, stringy-tough and burnt as brown as a boot by the Queensland sun. Not that Bob ever had boots on his feet, a shirt and shorts was all he wore. He'd spent his whole working life in one-cop outback places and he only ever had one method of dealing with troublesome people – step your frame outside and if you can knock him down you can go free, otherwise you get knocked down and told to go and yard yourself, which means you go and shut yourself in one of the cells down at the police station until Bob decides to let you go.

Some years after I left Queensland I got a letter from Bob, who'd recently retired. One of his last jobs, his letter said, was to go down to the Cairns hospital and interview two old codgers who'd been feuding over cleanskin cattle on the plains outside Cooktown for years. They'd hated each other for so long they'd forgotten how it started.

When Bob got down there these two old blokes were propped up in the same ward, each stonily ignoring the existence of the other. They'd taken three .22 bullets out of one of them and two .32 bullets out of the other, and they both swore black and blue that they were cleaning each other's guns and they'd gone off by accident. The rifles had been confiscated, the twenty-two was a single-shot.

"What's a bloke supposed to do, Crumpy?" Bob ends his letter.

It was Bob who asked us one day if we'd take some visitors shell-gathering. They were a retired Commissioner of Police from South Australia, his wife, and another couple. Them, Brother Bill, Jean and I set off in the *Waterwitch* for a cluster of coral bays called Three Isles, fifteen miles off Cape Flattery.

We anchored in the lagoon. The ex-policeman's wife was a bit seasick and we wanted to get her ashore and I didn't anchor the boat properly. I knew the anchor would probably pull off the small piece of coral I'd hooked it into and drag across into an underwater reef, where we might have to dive to dislodge it. That didn't matter.

As we got into the dinghy I told the ex-policeman he ought to stick a shirt on, but he said he was one of those people who never got sunburnt, he only went brown. Brother Bill and I glanced at each other and we rowed everyone ashore. Bill and I walked round the island, a couple of hundred yards, looking for Japanese glass fishing floats, which were washed up every-where on the coast around there.

When we got back to the others the ex-policeman had taken the dinghy and rowed out to the *Waterwitch* to get his shirt, and while he was on board the anchor pulled off the lump of coral it was on and the boat turned sideways and began to drift. It was still less than a hundred yards away. As we watched the ex-policeman came up from below and looked around, then he went forward and pulled in the anchor. We thought he must be going to start her up and bring her up towards the beach, but no. He sat on the cabin roof looking back at us and drifted out across the reef and out of the lagoon, while we shouted and waved and wrote COME BACK! on the beach.

For hours he could have even rowed back to us but he didn't seem to think of it. He went ashore that night on Flattery Beach, twenty miles of coral sand. Quite out of reach of civilization for the retired Commissioner of Police from South Australia.

The rest of us were worse off than him. He had water. We were stuck on a coral cay on the Barrier Reef without food, water or fire. Brother Bill and I knew that no one ever came out here. Anyone who could read a chart would see they didn't need to.

We spent the night burrowing into the warm sand at the top of the beach and in the morning we wrote S.O.S. on the beaches around the island and tied a red shirt on a pole to wave at any passing boats. Then the sun hit us and we knew we weren't going to be able to take much of this. Jean went looking for food on the reef and found oysters. Too salty to eat under the circumstances, but something to do. The other couple were pretty worried, but keeping it to themselves. The bloke was anxiously watching out for boats. The ex-policeman's wife came up to Bill and me demanding to know where her husband was, and to be taken home at once.

"Your old man's over there on the mainland with the wreckage of our boat, and if you don't get up there in the shade you'll be home a bit sooner than you bargained for," said Brother Bill grimly.

By next day we were getting really crook. Blazing hot and not a sign of any boats. They just didn't have any reason to come that way. We lay around in what shade we could find, unable to swallow or even talk. The ex-policeman's wife was whimpering and groaning under a shelter we'd made with broken-off mangrove branches.

Watching the horizon for boats that weren't coming. I remember looking across at Jean and thinking of all the things we'd done together since those crazy innocent coffee-bar days in Auckland. Now we were going to die together, and still she wasn't complaining.

It was Jean who saw the sail first. It was a yacht. It sailed straight past the island, a few hundred yards away from us. Shouting out was impossible but we ran round in slow motion and waved our red shirt and our arms. The bloke at the helm had his back to us, he sailed right past, and just when it was getting too late he turned his head, looked at us and turned away. Then he suddenly looked back again. He'd seen us! The yacht turned into the wind and three other blokes came on deck. We were saved.

They anchored in the lagoon and took us aboard in their dinghy. Four young New Zealanders, sailing around the world in a yacht they'd built themselves, the *Tuarangi*. It was a while before we could talk or drink water properly, or believe we weren't going to die after all.

It was decided that we'd better sail over to the mainland and see what had happened to the *Waterwitch* and the ex-police-man. And there she was, up in the breakers, water breaking in the stern and spuming out through the hatches. She'd had it. And there was the ex-commissioner of police from South Australia waving frantically on the beach. He had our dinghy upside-down for shelter.

"Give me a rifle!" pleaded Brother Bill.

There was no way we could land on that shore, and there were at least two crocodile rivers and miles of mangrove swamp between the ex-policeman and anyone else, except us. Brother Bill was inclined to leave him there but we anchored on the northern side of Cape Flattery and the next day Bill and I and two of the blokes from the yacht climbed across the cape and down to the beach on the other side.

The tide was out and the *Waterwitch* was lying on the sand, a wracked and broken hulk. Our books and stuff were washed up all along the beach. Nothing worth saving. All I took was the wooden nameplate off the *Waterwitch*. The ex-policeman was a bit indignant about us having taken so long to get there. He'd saved all their stuff and brought it with him in a sleeping bag sheet. He looked like Father Christmas ploughing along behind with his bag of gear.

It's a long hot climb to the top of Cape Flattery and by the time the ex-policeman came sweating up to the top of the ridge where we were waiting for him he was pretty bushed.

Y can't carry this any further," he gasped. "Mum's not going to be very pleased, but I've got to jettison some of it."

And he started fishing stuff out of his bag, a nightie, a pair of slippers, binoculars, some socks, and a large stainless steel chamber-pot. No kidding!

Brother Bill and I looked at each other. Everything we owned was washed up down there on the beach, and this bloke, who'd wrecked our boat and nearly killed us, was carting a pisspot across Cape Flattery.

"The Melbourne Cup!" shouted Brother Bill, and we both cracked up in hysterical laughter, rolling around on the sand.

It took Jack and his men thirteen hours, tacking against the Trade Winds, to get us back to Cooktown. They put us off at our jetty and had to get back out over the bar because the tide was dropping and they'd already lost enough time. As they cast off I stood on the jetty and said to Jack,

"I don't know how I'll ever be able to thank you, mate."

A quarter of a century later he was going to say exactly the same thing to me.

With no boat of our own any more Bill and I started going out with one of our mates, Lester, on his boat. It was decided that a bunch of us from Cooktown would camp on Lizard Island and trail for the big fish along the outer edge of the reef. There were Lester and his wife and three kids, Johnny Kane, Cubby the Abo, Brother Bill, Jean and me. Ten of us, on a thirty-foot boat, off to Lizard Island, fifty miles or so to the north of Cooktown.

It was a real pretty place, Lizard Island. I believe it's a tourist resort these days, but then it was unspoiled. Sandy beaches, palm trees, native bush, lagoons and coral reef. The kind of thing you read about. We set up a camp in a grove of trees by a freshwater spring, fifty yards or so back from the beach.

In this idyllic setting things went wrong from the start. Firstly a gear on Lester's boat chewed out. It was a gear that slipped over an eight-inch spline and was the main drive. And we had no radio.

Brother Bill decided to try and make a replacement gear. He cut the ends out of a diesel drum with a cold-chisel and drilled four holes in them with an eggbeater drill and bolted them together and marked out the gear and we drilled and cut it out with a hacksaw and a ten-inch file.

It took us days and we all had blisters on our hands from the hours of hacking and filing we'd had to do. After half a day of touching it up we got the new gear to slip onto the spline okay, but by this time the batteries were flat. We couldn't start the motor.

Brother Bill came to the rescue again. With the vee-belt off we could get a turn and a half round the main pulley with a thin rope, which we passed up through a pulley on the mast. Brother Bill crouched over the motor with a row of assorted knives under the tappets to take a bit of compression off her. Johnny Kane got ready to jam the leads on and get the last bit of grunt out of the batteries.

Brother Bill shouted "Right!", and Jean and Cubby and I jumped off the wheel-house roof into the sea, holding the rope that was round the pulley. Johnny Kane hit the starter and Bill played tricks with his row of knives. On the third attempt she fired and stopped. We knew we could do it and we kept it up until the motor started. We slipped the vee-belt on and left it running all night to charge the batteries up.

There's a bit of difference between being on holiday at a place and being trapped there. Some of them had started wanting to go back to Cooktown. We'd been getting a bit of blustery rainy weather. Ten people go through more tucker than you'd expect, too. We needed more supplies already. It turned out that everyone except me and Lester wanted to go back. That suited us, it only took the two of us to run the boat.

Jean and I had been getting a bit scratchy with one another just lately and we both realised that a bit of a break was a good idea, but we couldn't have guessed what kind of a break it was going to be. Jean had our camp on the jetty and plenty of friends and things to do. She was okay. Brother Bill and Johnny Kane were talking of going tin-scratching over at Mount Poverty.

Lester took them back to Cooktown. He was to load up with supplies and come back, and he and I would start filling the freezer on the boat with fish. I couldn't be bothered with the trip and stayed on the island.

They took off. The gear we'd made worked okay. In fact I heard that it lasted for two or three years and finally chewed out when they'd repossessed the boat and were taking it back down the coast to Brisbane, and she went up on the rocks at Princess Charlotte Bay.

As they were leaving Cubby pushed the dinghy back towards the shore for me and threw its anchor into it, a flywheel off a small motor, and it went straight through the bottom of the boat. The dinghy wasn't much use to me after that. I managed to patch it up a bit but I couldn't get very far in it.

I had a bit of food, and a .22 and .303 rifles, some spears – even a gill-net. Flocks of Torres Strait pigeons flew over from the mainland every day to feed in the trees on the island. They were good eating. There were quite a few turtles and small fish around the lagoon. I shouldn't have been able to go hungry there. But I did.

Two days after the others left a cyclone hit the place and roared up and down the coast for about a week. Then after two or three days another one came lashing through. Terrific winds, you could hear them coming like something moaning, and rain so heavy it built up on the ground faster than it could run away. I hoped Lester hadn't set out for Lizard when that lot hit us.

Suddenly there was no food around. The pigeons stopped coming out to the island and the turtles and fish all disappeared out into deeper water. The last food I ate was some honey in water, and then there was just water, heaps of it, pouring out of the sky, stinging in the wind, roaring in the leaves, running across my feet, beating up the surface of the lagoon. I wandered around in it as though it was there all the time. I'd been sleeping in a canvas hammock slung between two trees but in this rain it'd fill up in minutes, so I crouched among the roots of a huge tree with it over me and the rain roaring onto it. They were long nights. Wet clothes got a bit clammy and cold so I'd abandoned my shorts and got around naked.

When the rain came millions of tiny green frogs came out of the ground or somewhere. Millions of them. I got so used to squashing them underfoot I didn't notice any more, and whenever I picked something up I automatically shook the frogs off it. There was a row of dead frogs at the high water mark. And they had the most irritating squeak, like an unoiled gate-hinge. It was like a constant shriek, day and night. They weren't pleasant company at all, especially when they started sounding like voices in the wind.

I wasn't the first to have been stuck on Lizard Island, there were the remains of a small stone shelter and a brass plate in memory of a gutsy woman called Mrs Watson, who'd escaped with three children from a bunch of cannibals on one of the islands to the north. She got away in one of the big cauldrons they boiled whale-blubber down in and drifted onto Lizard, where she hung on for months until she was picked up by a passing boat. I hoped she hadn't had to endure those frogs.

More days went by, I lost track of them. And the weather was still very dickery, gales and heavy rain. I knew that no one was going to get to me while this weather kept up. I didn't know if I was going to last it out.

It had been blowing and raining on and off during the night and I'd got a bit cold so I went down and sat in the sea where it was warmer. As it began to get daylight the wind dropped and it stopped raining for a while. And I thought I heard a clanking sound. I'd been hearing and seeing some pretty far-out things just lately so I didn't take any notice of it. Then I heard the same thing again and turned my head and saw an ocean-going freighter in my lagoon.

This was impossible, and very disturbing. I tipped the water out of the dinghy and started rowing out towards the apparition, expecting it to disappear at any moment. But it didn't. It was the *Darega*, bound for Port Moresby with a load of bull-dozers and stuff. They'd put in for shelter from the cyclone, and getting a ship that size through the entrance to that lagoon was the smartest bit of seamanship I ever knew of. At night, too! They had no more than a few feet to spare, under and around them. They must have been real keen to get in out of that weather.

By the time my sinking dinghy bumped against the side of the ship someone on board had seen me. I wasn't very fit and two blokes gave me a hand to climb up some netting and onto the deck. Then they took me to the captain on the bridge. I was a bit embarrassed about being naked and asked for a pair of strides. Hadn't been expecting visitors.

The crew were good to me and gave me clothes and food. The first meal they stuck in front of me was a huge plateful of corned beef, cabbage, and boiled potatoes. I could do little more than sit there smelling it and looking at it. It was a few days before I could eat properly. I asked the captain if he'd let me have some supplies but he refused. Reckoned he'd be guilty of marooning a man if he left me there, and he'd never marooned a man and he was never going to. I would have to go to New Guinea with him and make my way to wherever I wanted to go from there.

That was fine with me. I'd never been on a boat this big and I'd never been to New Guinea. As long as I had a pair of pants on I was okay. We got through on the radio with a message to let Lester and Jean and them know what was happening, and waited for the weather to lift. Two of the crew bailed out my dinghy and rowed ashore to have a look around and came back freaked-out by the frogs.

It was some days before the weather began to settle. We manoeuvred the ship out of the lagoon and through a passage in the outer reef and I was off on another adventure.

When we got to Port Moresby Captain Houffe and I were officially placed under arrest, him for bringing an illegal immigrant into the country and me for being one. Unofficially we were treated very well indeed. The Red Cross bloke had been waiting for years to dress me up in shorts, long socks, shoes, shirt – the works.

The press had been waiting for us too. About twelve reporters crowded around asking all about it, interviewing the crew of the *Darega* and so on. We could only tell them the facts, but I saw that one of them reported that my mate had abandoned me on the island and didn't come back for me. They're beauts, some of those journos!

One of the reporters on the *South Pacific Post* was a mate of mine from Masterton. He put me up in his house and lent me some money and showed me around. I was Roger's best man at his wedding in Auckland a few years later.

Roger had this manservant who looked after the house and cooked and washed for him. He was a young bloke called Guari Fafa, and he took his job very seriously, too seriously. I had one shirt, one singlet, one pair of shorts and one pair of socks, and every time I took them off Guari Fafa would whisk them away and wash them. It got that way that if I couldn't find something I'd go out and get it off the line and put it on wet.

I couldn't get used to the idea of having a servant. I'd have liked to have seen some of the Europeans I met try talking to some of the Maoris I knew the way they talked to their Papuan servants.

I'd sent a cable to my publishers asking them to send me some money, but the only one who could authorise it, my editor, was away somewhere. There was a hold-up. Meanwhile one of my new friends lent me a jeep to get around in and I cruised the few miles of road there, checking out the Papuans.

The Collector of Customs, to whom I had to report, told me they'd been in touch with some embassy or other in New

Zealand, who'd told them I was a 'man of substance'. I thought that was a bit funny at the time because I was as skinny as a rake and as broke as you can get. Anyway I didn't have to report to the Collector of Customs every day after that.

I was up at the Kokoda Trail one day, wandering through a rubber-tree plantation, when four or five Papuans came out of the bush ahead of me carrying a dead person on a pole. They walked right past me, quite unconcerned. One of the women carried the guts in her skirt gathered up at the front. I circled back to where I'd left the jeep and trickled back to town.

In the few weeks I was in New Guinea I had a good look round and got to know a few of them. They're about the same as anyone else would be in the same circumstances. They chew betel-nut and spit red on the ground. We blow tobacco smoke into the air. But that dead person on a pole shook me a bit. Hard-case hearse.

An air ticket to New Zealand and some money arrived. They must have assumed that I wanted to go back there. By the time I'd paid Roger back the money I'd borrowed off him there wasn't much left, so I shouted my new friends a party before I left and arrived in Auckland with the clothes I stood up in and a bit of Australian change in my shorts pocket. I rang Cooktown a few days later to check on Jean. She'd gone off with a bunch of people to search for Lassitter's Lost Reef in the red heart of Australia.

I hadn't realised it – I don't think I even knew it was happening – but my new book was being launched at the same time news of my rescue from Lizard Island reached New Zealand. There was quite a splash in the press about it, with quite a few variations of the facts. One reviewer suggested that I'd got myself stuck on that island for a publicity stunt. I wished an hour of Lizard Island frogs on him.

The book sold out and has gone through a fair few editions since then. It was translated into Russian and sold a hundred thousand copies in that country. When I think about it, it must have been pretty good pay for five days' and nights' work, sitting in an armchair in Guy Powell's flat in Kelburn. Even roubles, if I ever want to go there and spend them.

Around this time I wandered into the back bar of the St George Hotel in Wellington and saw a strange-looking bloke, about fifty or so, with long hair and wearing a big cape. Never seen anything quite like him. He was telling jokes to about a dozen students. I edged along there and one of his jokes reminded me of one I knew, we told jokes and drank beer for two days and nights. Our audience grew and came and went in shifts as we moved from the pub to his place and back again. It was the most hilarious joke-telling session I ever knew. We were blue with ballpoint pen all over our hands and forearms from jotting down key words of jokes we remembered while one was being told.

I moved into his flat in Kelburn and we lived together for a couple of years and became lifelong friends. He was Erich Geiringer, the greatest humourist I ever knew. He was also an excellent doctor, not that I know anything about medicine, but you could tell. He cared. He explained things to you.

We got up to our fair share of harmless mischief, the eccentric doctor and the young writer from the bush, grooving around Wellington in my drop-head Jaguar or his dilapidated Mini. Good days. Heaps of laughter. I did some writing and Erich wrote the first NZ Medical Journals, dictated mostly from in the bath, shouted out to his girlfriend (later his wife) in the main room, and run off on a wind-the-handle machine.

More than a hundred women were dying every year in this country from cervical cancer, the second most-common cancer in women. It's a hell of a way to die and there's no need for it. Erich approached the Minister of Health and a good few other medical high-ups, suggesting an educational programme advising the women to have smear-tests. He ran into nothing but beaurocratic brick walls, such as doctors aren't allowed to advertise, it's unethical – stuff like that.

So we got some literature printed and flew to Dunedin and set up office in the bar of the Bowling-Green Hotel and got a bunch of students from the Medical School to put pamphlets in every postbox in Dunedin stating that there were 120 women in that city with unsuspected cervical cancer and all the women should see their doctor for a smear-test. On the Friday night we got them to hand out more information on the streets. The pavements were littered with our yellow pamphlets. Then we waited. We'd made some pretty extravagant claims and I was a bit nervous of the outcome.

I needn't have worried. In the ten days we were in Dunedin we found many more than 120 cases of unsuspected cervical cancer. I'm not sure if my memory is right but I seem to remember that we found around four hundred of them. Very curable in the early stages. We'd saved lives!

After that Erich's cancer campaign was recieved with much more tolerance and smear-tests became common and accepted. The only outfit that rejected his claims outright was the National Women's Hospital crowd in Green Lane. Years later the doctors at that hospital were the subject of a very heavy inquiry into their disgraceful attitude towards cervical cancer prevention.

Erich undoubtedly saved many lives with his campaign to make doctors and their patients know about cervical cancer prevention and yet he was never paid or acknowledged for it, he never expected to be. It needed doing so he done it. And that was just one of his incredible stunts. Great bloke, Erich!

My next adventure was six weeks on a film crew down the West Coast. I played the part of a crazy hermit. It was my first experience of film work and I've never liked it much. Too much waiting around doing nothing. Interesting though.

I met Selwyn Muru, the Maori painter, on that job and when it was over we moved into a flat in Wellington and he painted paintings and I wrote writings and we had many good times together.

Jean arrived back in Wellington. They'd failed to find Lassitter's Reef. She'd been working on an outback station in Western Australia. We slept together once and after all those years, she got pregnant. She rented a house in Wellington (which she later bought), wrote a book about our adventures called *Stand in the Rain* and had a son, named Harry after the bloke who first took us croc-shooting.

Jean's written several books since then. *The Balloon Watchers*, *Flowers from Happy-ever* and *Address to a King* are three I can think of. I reckon she's one of the best New Zealand writers we've ever had. There's a haunting kind of quality in the way she puts the words together.

CHAPTER SIX

In the mid-sixties I moved to Auckland and lived in eleven different one-room flats that I can think of. For some reason I've never been able to hit it off too well with city landlords and ladies, I seem to worry them. My working life ran a bit smoother and was a lot more fun. I got into doing interviews and skits for the producer of a television show called *Town and Around* and learnt not to worry about the camera.

I did some fairly hard-case interviews in those days. A friend recently reminded me of the time the head of a major English publishing-house (it might have been Collins) arrived in Auckland and because I had written books the producer asked me to interview him in the studio. They introduced us and sat us down and cued me to start,

"What's the guts of this publishing caper you're into, me old mate?" I said. "Tell us a bit about that."

I don't remember how the rest of the interview went, but there had to be a laugh in it.

Television was new here then and it was all go. I still reckon that some of the best local television we've had yet was done back in the old black-and-white days. None of us knew what we were doing but we were having fun doing it, and in that respect making television material seems to me to be a bit like writing. If it's fun to do, it's fun to watch. Laboured writing usually turns out hard to read. With me it does, anyway.

During this time I got some royalty money and bought a thirty-five-foot launch, *The Sunray*, and lived on board, moored in the Tamaki river. Between TV work I spent my time based at Great Barrier Island, long-lining for snapper in the Hauraki Gulf to make some money. We interviewers were getting fifteen dollars an item, and there was no way you could live on that.

That programme ran for a couple of years and then they changed things around and axed it. I'd picked up enough about filming work to be at ease with it. In fact ever since then I've liked the idea of getting a camera crew and cruising the highways and byways of New Zealand and filming the adventures as they happen. But the TV people always wanted a script before they'd commit any budget to it. No courage.

When *Town and Around* was discontinued I wrote and acted in a kids' programme called *Yo-Heave-Ho*. It was all done in the studio, good experience. There's nothing so intimidating as being interviewed in a television studio when you're unfamiliar with that atmosphere. They axed that programme too, but by the time they did I'd had enough of it.

I was getting bored with city life and moved away to the Bay of Plenty, but just before I left a young lady came around to my flat and told me she was three months pregnant. And it was me. And her old man came up from the South Island to say, "What are you going to do about it, Sport?"

I took her with me and we lived in a cottage in Te Teko and got to love one another (we didn't mind each other in the first place), got married and had two sons. I also assembled a pack of dogs and got back into hunting and fishing and jet-boating and guiding tourists. When we were living there I wrote and recorded a song called *Bad Blue*. As songs go it was no hit, but it's a good thing to have done.

A real bad thing, a tragedy, happened at Te Teko. A bunch of us started running a boys' camp in the bush behind Matahina. It was a success from the start. The right kind of roughing it. Great value for the boys, they really enjoyed it, they'd never done anything like that in their lives. Tramping, hunting, fishing, jet-boating and stuff like that.

We had about eighteen boys there at the time. I'd got used

to taking on the younger boys, nine and ten-year-olds, and the others handled the older boys, up to sixteen or seventeen. We'd been out spotlighting and I got my lot back to the camp and fed and into their bunks by about eleven o'clock. Some time in the early hours of the morning a farmer arrived at our camp on his tractor to tell us there'd been an accident. The other Land Rover had gone off the road into the lake and some of the boys were trapped in it.

Five of the boys were drowned. Five bodies to retrieve from the black waters of Lake Matahina and take into the morgue at Whakatane. Five lots of distraught parents to visit, five funerals to attend. Then the investigations and legal and news media stuff. It was a hell of a time and because my name was well-known I copped a fair bit of gossip over it.

It was no one's fault. Their Land Rover wheel had hit some fallen rock and one front wheel had gone over the edge of the road and then the whole vehicle slid twenty feet or so down through some scrub and rocks into the lake. The body wracked and the doors wouldn't open. Could have happened to me a hundred times.

One of my own sons who was at that camp was supposed to have been in that Landrover. There was nothing I could have done about that either. I feel for the parents of those boys whenever I think about it, though I've never felt in any way responsible for that accident.

After two years at Te Teko we moved to Waihi, where I trapped possums and wrote. Life was easy. Too easy. I'd been getting bored with being successful. It sure had its points but it hadn't answered any of my questions. Even a new station-wagon was a sterile pleasure. There had to be more to life than this. We surely weren't on this planet just to hassle each other for money and die. I was restless.

Not that there was nothing happening. Tex Morton, Jon Zealando and The Great Benyon all came and stayed with us and put on shows in Waihi, and it was fun getting to know and work with them. Tex Morton and I did several shows and some TV work, and Jon and his family became lifelong friends. Colourful, interesting people. Troupers! I remember one Friday night we slung Jon from a thirty-foot crane, handcuffed and in a straitjacket, in the main street to advertise his show that night. Packed the hall. Tex Morton got his stage name from the sign on Morton's garage in Waihi. I don't remember what his real name was.

All very exciting, but in a way I wasn't very excited. A friend persuaded me to have a go at golf, which I took up with enthusiasm. Out at the golf course and practicing drives so early in the morning that I had to wait for daylight to pick up the balls. By the time anyone else arrived to play with I'd usually done eighteen holes and was ready for a game, then another round if anyone was keen enough.

I never got under a sixteen handicap and golf failed to cure my restlessness, but I was glad of the experience because just after that I found myself ringbolting in a golf club in Germany playing with three American army officers and using the King of Belgium's woods, and it was real handy to be able to swing them as though I knew what I was doing.

I wrote a book and had it printed and published it myself, as much for the challenge of it as anything else. This one was entitled *Bastards I Have Met*. It sold out in two weeks and for the first time in my life I had some real cash in my kick.

My wife and I and the two kids stuck ourselves on a passenger-liner to England, where we stayed in London with my good friend Kevin, who was working on the *Times* newspaper. I liked London, with its lanes and pubs and colourful people, and all its other crazy goings-on.

I had a hard-case little adventure in London. A lot of people were wearing hippy-type gear but I'd never been game to, I'd have been recognized. But here I felt nice and anonymous. I went down town and bought myself a pair of flared jeans and high leather boots and a thin cotton shirt with a big sunflower on the front and a peace sign on the back and a big felt hat.

I was wandering through Picadilly with my ordinary clothes in a shopping bag, trying to catch my reflection in shop windows. Then I heard someone call out, "That's Barry Crump!"

It was a whole Kiwi rugby team, by the look of them. I was sprung! I snuck away down a lane and changed back into my usual clothes in a public toilet. You can't get away with it that easy. The boots were the only part of that outfit I ever wore again.

While I was in London I went to the Russian Embassy and enquired about royalties for a book of mine they'd published. Yes, it was okay to collect the royalties, providing I went to Russia and spent the money there. Then they provided me with an itinerary that scared me off the whole idea.

From London we went to Germany where a mate of mine was running a golf course for the American army. We stayed in a place called Garmish, not far from Munich, and toured around Europe in a converted bread-van we bought off a bloke called English Jim. Germany – France – Italy – Spain – Morocco – Lichenstein – Andorra – back to Germany, stay there for a while and then off for a look around somewhere else.

I heard a funny thing in Switzerland. We've got mountains in New Zealand, but Switzerland is *all* mountains, beauts! We'd been winding our way up a vast mountainside for miles and the van was overheating. Near the top of the range there was a big pull-over area and we stopped there to let her cool down a bit.

Across the gorge from us was a hugh glacier, thousands of feet of jutting blue and broken ice, the top of it lost in the cloud, and the bottom out of sight in the chasm below us. A truly awe-inspiring sight.

We were standing there looking at it when two tourist buses pulled in and all the people got out. It was obviously one of the sights on their tour. And among the "Ohh's" and "Ahh's" I heard a distinctly Kiwi accent (my guess'd be from around Otago or South Canterbury) say,

"She'd be a basterrd to musterr!"

I got a real grin out of hearing that, especially after having heard nothing but foreign accents for months. We didn't introduce ourselves, we got back in the van and off to Austria.

And back to Germany. We'd skimmed through most of Europe by this time. It was all very interesting and educational, but I'd seen enough of it, and my wife and kids had done enough travelling for the time being. They took the van back to London to stay with Kevin. I had other plans.

With the van gone I had nowhere to camp, so I started spending a lot of time at the golf club my mate Jim was managing. It was a pretty elaborate outfit in the Bavarian mountains. It was leased by the American Forces for the recreation of senior officers. I was told they had a nuclear installation nearby at Oberammergau and everyone was very security-conscious. I had no right to be near the facility at all and Jim and I had to be a bit crafty to cover my presence there. A little bit of Kiwi bull goes a long way on these occasions.

I played on the course all the time we were round Garmish, and lived there for three weeks while I bought a BMW 750/5 motorbike and waited for some travel-papers to be processed. I'd read in a book on self-realisation that there was a type of Indian Yoga that was guaranteed to work as long as you did it. It

114

sounded like the kind of thing I was looking for, I was going to check it out. Meantime I was shacked-up in the Garmisch Golf Clubhouse, trying to keep my head down and preparing myself for a long ride through many strange countries on my bike.

We almost came undone on one occasion. I'd got real friendly with some of the American officers, they were interesting to talk to and we had many good times in the lounge after a round of golf and dinner. Some of our yarn telling sessions went on for half the night.

They'd organised a putting competition and some of them insisted that I enter it. The first prize was a silver cup with the name and rank of the winner to be engraved on it. There were trestles under the trees set up for a Mongolian Barbecue loaded with beef, chicken, veal, fish, a salad-bar and kegs and kegs of beer. All this was set up near the nine-hole putting green beside the clubhouse terrace.

There were a lot of people there I'd never seen before and they kept asking me awkward questions, like what outfit I was with, and how my R and R was going. I got Jim aside and suggested that I just disappear, but he said that could make it worse because my name was on the board and if I went they might start to wonder who I was. We decided that I should play carelessly and eliminate myself early and then disappear until it was over.

Some of the competitors were getting a bit sloshed on the German beer and although I didn't even try I fluked some rather impressive putts and found myself in the quarter-finals. It's hard to throw a game by just not caring if you win or not, and before I knew it I was in a play-off between me and a grizzled, pipe-smoking major, who was obviously everyone's favourite to win. Mine too!

All the attention was on us as we prepared to putt-off. If I beat this bloke they were really going to want to know who I was and what I was doing there. Jim pushed past me and hissed,

"Don't you dare, Crump! What the hell do you think you're doing?"

He thought I was doing it on purpose. I didn't mind getting into trouble myself, but Jim's career was on the line. I was so nervous I couldn't play either badly or well. I just had to hit the ball towards the hole and hope it would miss, and to my horror I won the second and third holes. The fourth hole was a putt of about twenty feet and my first stroke went six or eight feet and there was laughter, but my second putt dropped into the cup to halve it with the Major, who was trying to win as hard as I was trying to lose.

He beat me by two holes and there was much applause. People congratulated me on having put up a good struggle. If they only knew. Jim dragged me away by the elbow. "What the hell did you do that for?" he demanded.

"Just teasing you, Jim," I grinned at him. "Don't worry about it, mate. She'll be right!"

And it was. It turned out to be a great send-off party for my journey to India.

The snow was down to the treeline on the Zugspitz when I left Garmisch and rode off on the first leg of my journey. Made it to Saltzberg in Austria the first day and slept in a camping-ground, and in the morning I found that someone had cut a two-foot rip in my little tent and cut the wallet from around my neck and taken three hundred American dollars out of it and left the wallet lying on the ground outside the tent. There's some slippery customers around!

In Yugoslavia I was put off the road several times by trucks overtaking, completely ignoring my presence on the road.

116

They prang, too. Burnt-out wrecks of cars and trucks and buses along both sides of the road. They just leave them there.

It's funny the things you remember about a place. One of the things I remember about Yugoslavia was watching a woman sweeping the tiled floor of a camping-ground restaurant, where I was waiting for a meal. There were thirty five tables and more than a hundred chairs, and she swept the whole place out with a straw broom without moving a single chair or table. She swept around all those table and chair legs, five hundred and forty of them. It took her more than half an hour.

On to Sofia, in Bulgaria. I was enjoying this. Every day when I pulled my boots on I was aware that when I took them off again I would have seen and done things I'd never seen or done before. Everything about me seemed to be black and silver. My clothes were all dark and the bike was black and silver. People were always speaking to me in German. I must have looked like one. I didn't mind being a German for a while. Change from being Barry Crump. I was losing weight, too, thinner than I'd been since Lizard Island. It was almost like being someone else.

In Sofia I had a go at finding a bloke who was wanting to put some of my writing in an anthology of world humor he was compiling. Svetoslav Kolev, his name was. He was a professor of languages at the Sofia University and should have been easy enough to find, but it was so hard to get to him I gave up on it in the finish and shot through. I don't know if Svetoslav ever knew I tried to find him.

Lousy roads in Bulgaria. The Bulgarians shake their heads for 'Yes' and nod them for 'No'. It's hard to get reliable directions from them.

In a small town fifty Ks or so from Sofia I hit a two-foot

117

trench they'd dug across the road. I flipped into the air and the bike came down on top of me. A handlebar dug into the road between my arm and my chest and the crash-bar landed between my legs and the bike rolled away without hurting me. Amazingly it was still running so I got up and picked it up and rode away.

Some workwomen in blue smocks who were drinking from tins besides the road there must have thought it was a pretty hard-case act. There was no sign warning traffic of road works and no one tried to flag me down, they just stood there and watched me ride up and smack into it.

In Istanbul in Turkey I found the noisiest, most hectic traffic I'd ever seen. Most of the tourists at the camping ground were afraid to drive their vehicles into town. He's a hard man, the Turk.

A taxi driver treated me to a hair-raising experience. He crossed into the opposite lane of the motorway and drove upstream among speeding traffic, cars, buses, trucks, weaving from one lane to another, then shot up an alley packed with people, to get me a loaf of bread. He got us back across the motorway by the same terrifying method.

"You must look the other driver in the eyes," my taxi driver confided to me, " or he might crash into you."

I haven't tried it out for myself yet.

I had a look around the bazaars and the Blue Mosque and an old palace, and moved on. The roads outside Istanbul were covered with carpets. New ones. Trucks and cars, horses and carts, all the traffic running across carpets, to make them look old so they could sell them as antiques.

The Turks had made a car with a fibreglass body, and one of the first crashes the police and insurance investigated had them stonkered until they discovered that the goats that ran around there everywhere had eaten half the shattered fibre-glass body off the car.

It's a very nice place to have a look around in, Turkey. Goreme – Derimkuyu, real interesting. The roads wind across the tussocky Turkish countryside as though they were drawn there by a child with a pencil.

I was cruising my way down a stony valley dotted with yellow and gold trees when a truck, bursting at the seams with people and gear and emitting high-pitched music and a cloud of black diesel-smoke, swerved around a corner and jammed me against the bank, then changed down and took off, quite unconcerned about the infidel on the bike.

I got a grazed leg and the clutch-lever got broken off. There was a bit of other damage, but they were the main things. I got the bike going, but riding a shaft-driven bike without a clutch sure teaches you how to get your revs right if you want to change gear. About a week later in Ezerum I got an 'engineer' to drill a hole in the stump of the clutch-lever, into which I jammed a four-inch nail. It soon worked loose in the alloy of the lever, but by only using it to start off with and in emergencies it lasted nearly all the way to India.

Into Iran, Ancient Persia. The further east I was getting the better I felt. Everyone I met seemed friendlier and even more helpful than the last.

Tabriz, magical place! – Tehran, where the traffic was something else again. When a hurtling taxi appeared an inch from my knee I had to be careful not to panic and swerve into the one an inch from my other knee.

Sari – Bodjnoord – Mashad, fantastic towns and countryside. Another world. Beaut road-bike cruising!

There's some pretty persistent salesmen in that part of the world. A bloke in Mashad made me agree to buy a 90,000-real carpet off him. I agreed to meet him the next day with the money and pick up this huge orange and blue carpet, to get him out of my ear.

The next day I was in Harat, in Afghanistan. Some of the weaponry for sale in the shops here was a bit sobering. Knives of every description, and rifles so old I would have been very chary about discharging any of the ones I saw. Swords and pistols displayed among the beads and embroidery on sale to the tourists. A chicken-gullet stuck on the wall of an eating house. They're a casual lot, the Afghanis.

I had a freaky adventure in Afghanistan. When I came through the border they were telling the tourists that there was some trouble with the locals. The hill-folk had cut two tourists' throats as they slept in their tent, and they hadn't taken anything, which was regarded as a bad sign. We could go through if we liked, but don't stop anywhere out on the road. They wouldn't take responsibility.

Between Harat and Kabul there's a good tarsealed highway passing through fantastic scenery. And during the journey I needed a leak, so I kept an eye open for a place where I could ride off the road into the desert, out of sight of the road. I finally found one and rode out into the desert and propped the bike up on a flat stone in a little hollow. I'd just taken my gloves off when I looked up and saw a bloke standing there with a gun. A home-made gun.

There were eight of them. All armed with guns and knives.

I pointed to my mouth and said, "I'll just have a bit of something to eat and get off your land if you like, mate."

I might as well have told them that Little Bo-Peep had lost her sheep. They just looked at me for a bit and then one of them who seemed to be the leader waved me to come with them. I got on the bike and idled off across the desert, surrounded by an escort of wild men.

I was getting pretty scared as the seriousness of the situation sank in. I surreptitiously eyed their guns to figure out how they worked, in case I could get my hands on one later on. They were muzzle-loaders. I'd have given everything I had for my old .303 and a full magazine right then. I could at least have put up a scrap. I felt helpless.

After about an hour some black tents came into view at the foot of a low ridge. As we approached I saw a group of women and children scurrying away out of sight. I propped my bike up for what was probably the last time and followed my captors into one of the smaller tents, where they sat me on a pile of stinking, half-cured goatskins and came back with a filthy bowl containing some curds and bits of other stuff it was wiser not to try to identify. Naturally I ate it all up like a good boy. Two men stayed in the tent with me and when I'd finished they took the bowl away and filled it again. I was only just holding onto the first lot and had to wave the second helping away.

I expected them to come back and deal with me, but the two men came back into the tent dragging a woman and shoved her towards me. She stood there, covered from head to foot in a black robe. Even the slot for her eyes was covered in black lace. The only part of her I could see was her bare feet. She had a silver thing around one of her ankles.

I suddenly realised that these people were offering me this woman! I wasn't actually thinking of sex at all just then, let alone with someone from another planet. I waved her away and the two men grabbed her and threw her out of the tent as though she'd done something wrong and followed her out.

I began to think I mightn't be going to be pulled in half by wild horses after all. They'd given me food and offered me more, and then they'd tried to give me a woman. They'd also given me a fine crop of lice that crawled up out of the skins I was sitting on.

I went to the doorway and pulled the flap aside. Half a dozen wary-eyed men were squatting around a small fire near the tent. There were bunches of other people standing around. All the men had guns. My bike was still there, a ring of footprints in the sand around it, but untouched as far as I could see.

I went over to the men at the fire, who all stood up as I approached.

"Thanks for the feed," I said. "I think I'll take off now if it's all the same to you blokes."

They didn't move or say anything. I went over to the bike and got on it and started it up and rode slowly away, expecting everything to suddenly end with the slam of a bullet. My back was crawling, and it wasn't just lice. A hundred yards out into the desert I cautiously gave the bike a few more revs, their guns wouldn't have been good for much more distance than that. After a long time I realised I was in the clear. Too much in the clear, I had no idea where the road was. I was lost in the Afghan desert.

I must have been riding around for a couple of hours when I thought I saw a puff of diesel smoke away out to one side. It was the road. Very pleased to see it, too. I had just enough gas left, to get me to Kandahar.

A bloke I met in Kabul told me that I'd probably saved my life by asking the Afghani tribesmen for food. Their religion says that if a stranger asks them for food they must give it, even if they have to go without themselves. They also sit up in the hills, this bloke reckoned, and pray to Allah for the things western people have. Someone pulls up in a campervan for a cup of tea and the Afghanis bowl down to take delivery of it, praising Allah for his generosity, and dealing with anyone who tries to stop them. If that was true I'd had a pretty close shave that time.

There was an interesting sign in the Green Hotel in Kandahar, where I stayed a night. I copied it down in a note-book I was carrying and can give it to you verbatim.

FOR YOUR AVAILABLE THINGS THERE IS NO
MANAGEMENT GIVE TO THE MANAGER OF THE
HOTEL AND TAKE RECEIPT FOR IT OTHERWISE
YOU ARE THE RESPONSIBLE FOR YOUR STELF.
THANK YOU.
M.R.
(HOTEL MANAGER)

I was getting closer to India and beginning to think I might actually make it. In Pakistan I had an interesting accident, to look back on. It was in the Khyber Pass. The road was good and dry and I was swooping through the mountains like a big black and silver eagle, the bike humming smoothly in the heart of us. We would have been difficult to overtake.

In the midst of all this exhilaration I flew over a rise and there on the road in front of me was a whole tribe of people camped on the road. It wasn't a matter of whether I was going to hit anything, it was a matter of what I was going to hit first.

The decision was taken out of my hands. A truck or some-thing had bowled a cow there and killed it. These nomads had come across it and were cutting it up and cooking it. I was braking hard when my front wheel hit where they'd gutted the cow and down I went, the bike and I sliding right into them.

We bowled aside two people and sent flying a burning car tyre they'd been cooking strips of meat over, slid under the noses of two bullocks pulling a wooden-wheeled cart, took the legs and wheels out from under a bloke wheeling a pushbike with a load of empty tins tied on it, wiped the end out of a fruit and vegetable stall set up in wooden boxes, scattered a bundle of clothes and stuff someone had dropped, then slammed into a metal strip around the edge of a thousand-foot drop.

I was winded. I looked back up the swathe I'd cut through the lives of these peaceful folk going about their daily business and remembered someone saying that you should never stop if you prang any of the locals around here, they're liable to stone you to death.

At this stage this lot were still wondering what had hit them so suddenly. I crawled across to the bike and got it and me on our feet. We were both pretty grazed and bruised but we worked. I rode off down the hill keeping the speed down a bit. Another pair of jeans with the backside out of them.

I'd done those people back there a favour. I was a warning to them. I'd hate to have seen what would have happened if a decent-sized truck had come over that rise and ploughed into them.

Peshawar – Rawalpindi, the roads here were cluttered with an amazing array of traffic. Cars, cows, camels and people, buffalo, buses, bikes, beggars, dogs, donkeys, goats and garbage, to mention but some of it. The roads themselves were in shocking condition, I suppose they could never clear the traffic to do any work on them.

In Lahore I had a lucky prang. A cow walked out right in front of me and I couldn't avoid it. I knocked both it and myself aside and I ended up inside an eating-house in a tangle of chairs and tables and turbans and saris. No one else was hurt and a few rupees squared off the eating-house bloke, but outside it wasn't quite that simple.

The bike was halfway up the steps of the building next door and the crowd had thickened. I'd hit a cow, not a hell of a good

124

idea in this neck of the woods. The cows I were used to got out of your road, these people worshipped them. And they were getting pretty worked-up about me bowling this one, which was limping away surrounded by an excited babble of people. The crowd around me was pressing closer and sounding angrier all the time. I dragged the bike off the steps. I'd sprung a rib or two, which didn't make things any easier, I couldn't stand up straight. The nail was missing out of the clutch-lever and I needed to get a bit of a run-on to start the bike, but the people were crowding too close. I wheeled my way through them. Some of them plucked at my clothes but that was all they did.

The crowd gradually thinned out until two young blokes who obviously didn't know I'd just knocked a sacred cow over offered me a push. The bike started and I was away from Lahore.

And then Amritsa. I'd made it. I got through the border and rode my battered BMW into India feeling pretty good about life. And lucky. Lucky to have got there, but luckier still to have done it. It had taken two months. I'd ridden from Germany to India in less time than it had taken Jean and me to drive from Auckland to Wellington in the '34 Chev.

The bike was worth about half what I'd paid for it. The tank and exhaust pipes were scraped and dented. The headlight was a broken poultice of wire, no indicators, flasher, lights or horn. Half the front mudguard was broken off and the crashbar was torn off one side and the footrest bent back against the muffler. The clutch-lever and rear-vision mirrors were back in Turkey somewhere. The handlebars were twisted lower on one side and back on the other. Half the fins were broken off one tappet-cover and the front forks were bent and almost rigid. And she was still running like a dream.

At Amritsa I had a look around the Golden Temple. An

impressive thing indeed! I was struck by the depth of religious feeling and practices here. Sufis and Sikhs, Buddhists, Moslems, Hindus and other religious creeds, all intermingled and praying to the same God under different headings. These people couldn't be any closer and yet they shunned one another. They all meant it, though.

I wasn't here to see the cities and left Amritsa for Kashmir. I remember a little town on the way to Jammu with a main street like an obstacle-course for trail-bikes. Some of the holes were two and a half feet deep and filled with mud and water. You'd have bellied an ordinary car there. The only traffic round there seemed to be trucks, camels and donkeys.

On through Banihal. Great mountains, awe-inspiring. Clear rivers, like at home. This was some of the best bike-cruising I've done, ever. Climbing up and around and down the mountain-sides of this delightful part of the world. Through a mile and a half of unlit tunnel and down through a wide beautiful valley to Srinagar, on the shores of Dal Lake.

There'd been some rioting in Srinagar and there were Indian soldiers everywhere. They stopped me and told me that the town wasn't safe to stay in. The best thing I could do was stay in one of the houseboats across the lake. I wasn't going to argue with them. I locked my bike in a room behind a shop for ten rupees a week, took my saddlebags and got taken across to the *New Golden Hind* houseboat, in a shikara paddled by a small boy who was to have a more profound effect on my life than the guru I'd come all this way to find.

CHAPTER SEVEN

The *New Golden Hind* houseboat was comfortable and clean. It was moored to a tiny island out in Dal Lake. These islands, this one was about the area of a three-bedroom house, had been built up by the Kashmiris with canoe-loads of mud, because all their land had been taken off them and they had nowhere else to go but out into the lake, which was fortunately quite shallow. They lived in huts on the islands and some of them rented houseboat accommodation to the tourists, who lived much better than they did.

The family I was staying with were the Goosanis. Ramani Goosani and his wife, Gulam, twenty-two, the eldest son and his wife. They had a baby. Then there was Abdul, Fatima, the daughter, and Sheffy, a nineyear-old boy. They couldn't do enough for me. The women were very shy and stayed in the background.

There weren't many tourists around because of the rioting and the houseboat people were doing a bit of a starve. They hadn't asked me for any money yet so I offered Ramani a month's rent in advance and he almost wept as he accepted it. A shikara was dispatched to the town and returned with a whole sack of rice, flour, cabbages and other supplies. By the time I left there, about five months later, I'd paid him more than two years' advance rent. He was too proud to accept it any other way.

The odd tourist came and went but they didn't get in my way. There were three bedrooms on the houseboat. I settled into enjoying the place. There were a hundred miles of waterways and lakes to explore.

There was a wise man, a yogi, who was just then living in a cave up in the hills. When Gulam told me how to get there he warned me about a certain scrub-bush that grew around there. It seemed that if you sit near one for too long you become unable to get up and walk away from it. Someone had to come and lead you away or you'd sit there till you died. I'd heard a few other strange things about here but I was keeping my mind ajar about them. I never did find that wait-a-while bush.

The yogi's cave was up a rocky, scrubby track two hundred yards or so from the road. I passed a couple of turbaned men coming down the track and there were several others sitting around the entrance of the cave when I got there. It was more of an elaborate overhang than an actual cave.

The yogi was sitting on carpets with his feet in his lap. The top of his head was bald and he had long white hair hanging down from the sides of his head and a long white beard. He sure looked like a yogi. He had a nice face. He was talking to two young blokes sitting in front of him through an interpreter.

It was all Indian to me. I sat slightly apart from them, cross legged. After a while the two young blokes stood up and bowed to the yogi a few times and left. He waved me forward.

"You have travelled far to see me", he said in heavily accented English, motioning me to sit.

It was a funny interview, looking back on it. It went something like this.

"Yes," I replied.

"You have something to ask me."

"Do you know things I don't know?"

"Yes."

"Could you teach me?"

"Yes."

"How long would it take?"

"Four months, for you."

We were mad, neither of us had ever had anything to do with boats in our lives.

. . . and fishing and jet-boating.

A gaunt, shy stranger with a queer accent and the Chella throwing tantrums in my soul.

I'll always prefer radio. Disembodied voices from any distance or age, communicating with other voices.

We made some really close friends amongst the Cook Islanders.

A young pretender . . . I think the specs are a bit big mate!

We started getting flakes and specks of gold in almost every pan of gravel.

We slept in the Model-A.

Toyota gave us one of their utes. It could handle a bit more water than the Model-A.

Going for a hunt . . .

I did a stint as a cook for a merino-mustering gang in Otago.

Brought up around animals especially horses and dogs.

With Dame Whina and Sir Edmund Hillary at Government House, 1991.

"Would you do it please?"

"I will do it."

"What's first?"

"You must give me a hundred rupees."

"I've come to the wrong place."

"Sit down again. You have just passed my first test."

"What's next?"

"You must stop smoking tobacco."

"Okay. What's next?"

I already had an idea what was next. Sitting cross-legged is fine when you've been doing it all your life, but by this time I was almost ready for a double hip-replacement. He showed me how to sit straight and gave me some breathing exercises to do. That was all.

"When do I come back?" I asked him.

"I have other caves to visit. Come here again when the moon is three days past full."

I thanked him and left, my mind still ajar.

I enjoyed taking the small shikara and paddling around the lake with my firepot under my faran – that means that I had a small earthenware crock filled with embers from the fire under my new Kashmiri coat. The underwater plants reach nearly to the surface and the water is very clear and still. One stroke of the paddle can set you off on a silent quarter-mile glide across the top of a fascinating underwater jungle inhabited by strange creatures, slowly turning through the reflected image of towering snow-streaked mountains and clouded sky in an atmosphere like condensed moonlight. In other places your shikara shushes through half an acre of floating lotus-blossoms. It's a very spiritual flower, the lotus. In fact the whole darn place was spiritual, especially the people.

Or I might go the other way and paddle down an avenue of weeping-willow-type trees to one of the shops on piles at the water's edge and, standing up in my canoe, buy myself a mug of yoghurt or a flavoured biscuit, and then cruise round some of the more distant and primitive parts of the lake. It was basically the same everywhere. Happy industrious people doing what they had to do with what they had to do it with. I liked them.

Sometimes someone would start to sing as they paddled along and someone else would join in from further over, then someone else, until the whole area was being sung in. I wished I could join in. The place was getting to me.

The Goosanis were quite astonished at some of the places I'd paddled to around the lake, but then they hadn't been out harpooning dugong with Tarzan and Rosie in the Gulf of Carpentaria. How far away all that seemed now.

I'd been practicing my yoga exercises and could sit cross-legged long enough for most occasions. I was ready for the next step in my self-enlightenment by the time the moon was three days past full. I bent my steps to the cave of Yogaprana, for such was his name, and after the exchange of greetings I received my next instructions. I was to disembody.

Now, I'm game for just about anything, but I didn't like the sound of this. I wanted to know more about it. He explained. He himself could disembody at will and be anywhere he knew about, almost instantly, and then return any time he wanted. Using his methods of breath-control and thought patterns I did it myself, very clumsily, a few times. I could see that if you got good at it you could have a great time out there, but it wasn't what I was looking for. I couldn't see humanity solving its problems by everyone sitting around disembodying all over the place.

130

Yogaprana was fair-dinkum, though. He could do what he claimed. I visited him twice more, and paid him his hundred rupees. It was good value.

"Salam alaikom!"

"Salam, Saab!"

That took care of that, but it left me worse off than ever. I'd come all this way to try something and it hadn't worked. I knew that all the yogis weren't the same, but I didn't fancy my chances of running into one who could show me why we were all here in the first place. I was beginning to think that my whole journey might have been based on a dream. There was plenty of evidence to support that notion.

But while all this was going on the strangest thing was beginning to happen at home. I'd become closer to the Goosani family than I was actually comfortable with. The father, Ramani, and I were great mates. We laughed a lot, he was a happy man. His eldest son, Gulam, and I talked far into the night by our fire. Gulam had really clear brains and refreshing attitudes towards things. Like all the Kashmiris he was trapped in this valley and intensely curious about the world outside. He would laugh uproariously at some of the things I told him we did out there. It was hard for him to imagine how western society held together at all.

Abdul was always looking for something to do for me, Fatima, the daughter, was fifteen and very pretty and very shy. Young Sheffy looked after my firepot and the stove in the houseboat and fetched stuff. For his age, nine, Sheffy was a lot more capable and deft and responsible than the young blokes I was used to. The other women, Ramani and Gulam's wives, did most of the work and were very happy to do it, as far as I could see.

They made me move into their hut with them. I didn't particularly want to but they made me. I slept in one of the rooms with Abudul and Sheffy, under blankets on a thin mattress on the floor. I ate out of a bowl with my fingers, sitting cross-legged on the floor of the kitchen with the rest of them.

The kitchen was the main room. Cooking-fire in the middle of the room, smoke out through the roof. Dirt floor packed and baked and swept to a polish. Drum of water on a box, bowls and pots and stuff on a low shelf along one wall. Candlelight. I was no stranger to this atmosphere.

Every morning after our rice Ramani brought out the Koran. Ours was a big old one, on a low intricately-carved wooden stand, opened at the page we were on last time and covered by a lacy embroidered cloth. He placed the stand gently like a new-born baby on the floor and lifted aside the cloth as though it was revealing all the treasures of the world, and began to sing the words of Mohammed, the Messenger of God, pausing now and then to let the ecstasy pass when he came to a verse that particularly thrilled him.

It was highly infectious. I couldn't understand the words, neither could Gulam's baby, but we tingled with the sheer uninhibited joy of it the same as all the others. After twenty minutes or so of chanting, Ramani would come to a verse he couldn't get past, so carried-away was he. He'd read it again and then again and trail off, tearfully shaking his head.

"Oh Saab, it so beautiful" he'd say.

"Yes," I'd agree.

And we'd sit in silence for a while letting the atmosphere hum around and through us. Then Ramani would draw the cloth across the open pages of the Holy Book and take it into the other room and we dispersed to do whatever we were into that day. Sure took care of any getting out of the wrong side of the bed.

After the evening meal we'd build up the fire and sit around talking and singing and laughing.

132

Abdul begged me to let him wash my feet.

"No thanks, Abdul. I gave them a bit of a going-over in the lake today, thanks all the same, mate."

But he got so sad about it that I had to say okay in the finish. He got a basin of very hot water and dipped his fingers into it and began to trickle it over my calves and feet. Then as the water became less hot he gently massaged my calves and ankles and feet.

I couldn't help wondering what some of my deer-culling mates would have said if they'd sprung Crump sitting in a hut with another bloke massaging his feet, but that inhibition vanished with the wonderful feeling of relaxation and well-being Abdul gave me. Every night after our meal Abdul would order a basin of hot water from the women and massage my feet while we talked and sang.

"What does Abdul mean in English talk, Gulam?" I asked him one day.

"Servant," said Gulam, and we both smiled.

I'd been having a bit of trouble getting away on my own in the shikara without young Sheffy. I'd be barely thinking of going for a paddle around when he'd offer to be my paddle . . . show me where Mohammed's hair was hidden . . . watch out for bad people . . . show me where the magic water comes into the lake . . . take me to the Peligram . . . a secret temple no one knows about.

This day I let him paddle me. Paddling a canoe was like walking to him. We were gliding up an arm of the lake I'd never been in before. Some of the houses were built out over the water on poles. They were mostly fishing people here. They slide around the lake squatting on the front of their shikaras with a spear poised. Their main fish is like a silvery trout to look at and like muddy crayfish to eat.

133

"I'm be your Chella," said Sheffy.

"What's that?" I said.

"I fill your firepot, wash clothes of you, paddle shikara. Look after you."

"You do that already," I said. "What am I supposed to do in return?"

"You think to God for both of us."

"Is that all there is to it?"

"Sure, okay?"

"Okay," I shrugged.

But there was more to it than that. A hell of a lot more. I didn't know what I was letting myself in for. There was great excitement in the household that night when Sheffy told his family he was my Chella. Ramani squeezed my arm and made a speech about how I'd honoured his family, and his father's family and his father's-father's-father's families as well. He speeched again in Kashmiri for his wife and Gulam's because they didn't know English talk.

Abdul had to show the Chella how to do my feet properly. He was never as good at it as Abdul, but I suppose a man has to make some sacrifices.

It kept getting deeper. The responsibilities of having a Chella became more than I'd ever had with my own kids, or whole family for that matter. His name became Chella and I never heard anyone else in the community call him Sheffy again, except me, once, by accident. I got a hurt look and no other reply.

He had to have a new coat. He left school, that was my job. His parents and brothers relinquished all authority over him, and he began to order them around, especially his mother, something disgraceful. The situation would have completely ruined any other nine-year-old I knew, but Chella had an air of responsibility about him that was more than his new freedom and authority could undermine.

We had to eat out of the same bowl. He slept curled up against me. When I went into the lavatory at one end of our island he waited outside. When he wanted to go to the lavatory he'd touch the very spot on the ground where I was to stand and say, "Here you wait!"

If I'd kept my side of our bargain as conscientiously as Chella was keeping his, I'm sure we would have given God spiritual indigestion. I'd been loved by some good women but I'd never been attended to so constantly and energetically as this young bloke was laying on me. If he was a dog I'd have had to shoot him.

I was in the habit of visiting some of the Kashmiri people living round the lake some evenings, especially the old people. We often talked until well into the night, we had heaps to share. They jokingly called me The Unfolding Flower.

Now I always had the Chella sitting beside me, touching me if he could wangle it, getting up now and then to fill our fire-pot with embers from the fire or top up our tea-bowl from the samovar.

"Are *you* tired, Chella?" I'd say.

"Are you tired?" he'd say.

"No."

"How can I be tired? We're not tired."

Or "Are *you* hungry, Chella?"

"Are you hungry?" he'd say.

"I am a bit."

"We're hungry!" And he'd order his mother or Gulam's wife to get food.

Within a week the Chella's English had improved out of sight, with my accent. He was using words with my accent I

135

knew I'd never spoken to him. They were all keen to practice and improve their English. And I was slipping into some of their speech mannerisms. I wasn't hearing anyone speak English except with a Kashmiri accent, it was the only way they could understand it, and the Chella and I talked a kind of pidgin that I still slip into when I remember those times, because those time remember me very happy to my heart.

A passing tailor was called ashore and ordered to make me a Kashmiri suit. The whole family sat around watching him sew my new blue cotton suit on his old hand-cranked Singer sewing-machine. The Chella oversaw the whole operation with an air of authority that was embarrassing. No one seemed to mind him bossing them around on my behalf. I'd have given him a biff if I'd been them, but they actually seemed to be enjoying it.

The suit was like loose pajamas. It was the most comfortable clothes I've ever worn and after a week or two I couldn't imagine myself ever wanting or needing to wear anything else.

Gulam and Abdul took over looking after the tourists. Apparently it was quite out of the question for the Chella to do anything for anyone else but me. The tourists thought I was a Kashmiri until they heard me speak. I avoided them because when they discovered I was a tourist they wanted to know all about it, and I didn't know what to say to them.

By this time I was as shy of strangers as the Kashmiris themselves, so when we had tourists the Chella and I spent all day away round the lake. We had friends all over the place. I wasn't feeling so claustrophobic about having him so close around me by this time. I'd even got used to him helping himself to other people's embers for The Saab's firepot.

Those days were so easy-going they were unreal. The Chella's uncomplicated open-hearted happiness was infectious.

He'd get more fun out of a flimsy little paper kite on a reel of cotton than my kids would get out of a new bike. He taught me the songs he sang all the time.

Mera pichinar
Shore gorba dongeay,
Dor de loka, mel a mare
Baji-dajai, mel a mare.

I made him make me know what those words meant in English talk. It was some kind of nursery-rhyme.

I showed him how to write in English. He was astonishingly easy to teach. He filled my only notebook with his Arabic trained handwriting.

He had a very simple and practical approach to religion, the Chella. We were paddling along in silence in the moonlight one night. I was lost in wonderment at the majesty and beauty of the scenery around us.

"You thinking to God for us, Saab?" asked the Chella.

"In a way, yes," I said. "What you think about God, Chella?"

"God say man go in mud, man say okay!" he said.

Can't argue with that.

For months the Chella and I drifted through the waterways of Kashmir, eating water-chestnuts and rice, me telling him stories to make him know what the world was like outside his valley. I had to be careful to be accurate about what I said because he soaked it up and believed every word of it, and if there was anyone in the world I didn't want to put crook it was the Chella. He trusted me. Also it was getting hard to remember what it was like out there.

"Big buildings out there," I told him one day.

"How big?" he said.

"Twenty-two house one on one like that," I said.

"What for they do that?"

"Fit everyone on the island."

He thought for a moment and then he said, "What if God go – ," and he shrugged.

"They make it earthquake-proof," I said.

The chella looked up with disbelief at the mountains that towered above us and rolled back laughing in the shikara and splashed his paddle in the water, "I reckon they mad out there all right!" and we laughed across the lake about people who can make a truck and an aeroplane and make talk on the telephone through the mountains but still think God can't shake twenty-two house one on one.

The Chella's teeth were rotten, which was a bit unfortunate because he smiled a lot. They were giving him trouble and his breath was keeping me awake at night. We went over to the town and it was dark by the time I got him into the dentist's filthy, dimly-lit 'chambers'. The Indian dentist had a young girl sitting on a kitchen chair and was extracting her back teeth by the light of a kerosene lamp, wiping away the blood with a dirty towel.

There was a spare pair of teeth-pliers in a chipped white enamelled bowl of bloodied water on the bench there. For twenty rupees the dentist agreed to lend them to me for twenty hours. I took them home and got the Chella to make the women boil hell out of them. They'd been chromium-plated and some of the chrome was peeling away.

Next morning I got the pliers boiled again and took the Chella out in the light and pulled six of his teeth out. They were rotten. Some of his other ones were going to have to come out soon, too. It must have hurt him a fair bit but he hardly flinched. He'd have cheerfully let me break his leg if I'd wanted to.

I didn't notice anyone leave our island, they were all engrossed in watching the Chella's teeth being pulled out, but by the time I'd finished him, others were arriving, shikara after shikara, all with people with rotten teeth to be pulled. I'd sooner have harpooned an eighteen-foot salty than pull all those teeth, but I had to do it. Gulam, Abdul and Fatima all needed rotten teeth pulled. Ramani and the women had none left.

I got continuous boiling water going and one after the other – in an order dictated by the Chella – I pulled the rotten teeth out of their heads. Old men and women, middle-aged people, boys and girls and even little children. A couple of them were so bad I wasn't game to tackle them and sent them over to take their chances with the Indian dentist.

I'll bet I pulled more than a hundred teeth that day. Not bad for a first attempt. I found that the dentist only came up from New Delhi every three months or so, and he charged too much for most of us lake people. The Chella and I went over and haggled with him and finally bought the tooth-pliers off him for another forty rupees. We kept them on the kitchen wall with their special boiling-bowl on a shelf below them.

A steady trickle of people came to have their rotten and aching teeth pulled as word of The Saab Goosani reached further afield. They'd got the idea that I was a famous American dental surgeon and the Chella wouldn't tell them I wasn't. I'd tell him to make them know that they were in the hands of a Kiwi bushman, but judging by their reaction he might as well have been supporting the rumour. He had as much mischief in him as any other nine-year-old. I couldn't make them realise that where I come from a bloke could get into all sorts of strife for practicing dentistry without a ticket. I was too downright scared to take any kind of payment for tooth-pulling, but they didn't understand why, and it only added to my spurious reputation as a good bloke.

One day Gulam, the Chella and I were sitting there when a shikara passed across the lake about a hundred yards out.

"There is Habib," said Gulam getting to his feet. "We want to have talk with Habib."

We got into a shikara and paddled out to intercept Habib. Gulam whistled out a couple of times and the whistle was carried on across the lake. Several other shikaras put out and headed toward us, all with young men in them. Habib drifted to a stop and as we surrounded him he was looking decidedly uneasy.

"You still selling that hashish to those American hippies Habib," stated Gulam.

"What you do that for?" said one of the others.

"For money," said Habib.

He looked around us. We all shook our heads.

"Don't do that to us, Habib," said Gulam.

"You making us dirty," said someone else.

"You make my sister dirty," said his brother-in-law.

"You making The Saab dirty," said the Chella.

I nodded seriously.

"Not good, Habib!"

When we knew that Habib wasn't going to sell that hashish to those American hippies any more we left him to paddle on his way. A few days later he came past paddling the chemist's shikara-shop. He was looking much better. Cleaner. We had hashish-bush growing around but hardly any of our people ever smoked it. Makes you dirty.

Another day the Chella and I were picking our way through some huge slabs of broken rock on the crest of a ridge above the lake and we met a family of Tibetan people. There were seven of them, dressed like you see in photographs. They had a happy little baby in one of the panniers on a llama they were

140

leading, and they'd come through some pretty hectic country-side. Here were fair-dinkum mountain people. We clamber around in the mountains for sport, the Tibetans live up there all the time, they have to.

The Chella could talk some of their talk and we exchanged greetings. They were on their way to Srinagar to trade embroi-dery and other hand-crafts for rice and cloth. This was a spe-cial trip for them. They begged us to sit, and then reverently unrolled a canvas they had in their pannier and held up one of the most remarkable things I've ever seen. It was a silk robe, completely embroidered with the scene of a spectacular sunset in towering mountains. The intricate blending of the colours and detail were fascinating. The more you looked the more you saw. I felt wonderment that such a beautifully delicate work of human art had been produced in such a harsh and rugged place. It had taken an old man fourteen years to embroider it.

They held it up in silence for perhaps half an hour, while the Chella and I sat and explored it. Finally, "Our eyes are full, Saab," said the Chella.

I nodded and he ordered them to roll it up, and talk and laughter started up again. The ritual was over.

We walked along with our new friends, laughing and happy, like kids used to be on the way to the movies, excitedly clap-ping their hands at the sight of a bird or a lizard they weren't used to. They walk across broken rock like we walk across cow-ruts. We parted from them on the road to Srinagar and I never saw them again.

"They like me, Saab," said the Chella. He meant us.

Those Tibetans were the purest people I ever met. It's an honour to have stood near them. I don't know how much they got for their coat, but I do know what happened to it. I met the

American bloke who bought it off Subhana-The-Best for two hundred dollars. Subhana-The-Worst, his brother just along the road, would probably have stung him a bit more for it.

I cracked it for a chat with the American bloke and invited him to stay on our houseboat because we needed the money. Clem and I became good friends, although he only stayed a few days, and we've kept in touch ever since. He visited me once in New Zealand. I must write to Clem. I'd like to have another look at that coat, though I doubt that it would have the same effect on me these days as it did when I first saw it on that ridge above Dal Lake in Kashmir.

I asked Subharna-The-Best what he'd paid the Tibetans for the Coat, and what he told me added up to over three hundred dollars' worth, the lying old coot. I figured that the old man got less than a hundred dollars' worth of goods for his fourteen years' work. They were able to afford their first transistor radio, so maybe the bloke's labours weren't so cheaply disposed of after all.

It was meeting the Tibetan family that made me realise that I'd travelled from the oceans of materialism in the west, up the rivers and streams of desire and greed to the unpolluted springs and creek-heads in the mountains of the east. I wonder if it's true that the less you've got the easier it is to laugh.

One of our relatives, a cousin Lorin, was getting married to Haffi's daughter, the pretty one, and the preparations for the wedding made me not want to miss it. The atmosphere around the lake became romantic. Everyone seemed to be singing as they paddled around and splashed each other in passing, and gathered flowers, and prepared the food and the bride and the embroidered clothing, and decorated the donga that bore the bride's entourage in a blaze of coloured lights reflected across the water in a choir of singing.

There was singing and feasting for two days and nights. When a singer's performance pleased someone in the audience they'd get up and pin some money on them for the couple. Some of the singers were covered in notes by the time the newlyweds poled away across the lake in their little houseboat. I decided then that if I ever got married again I was going to insist on a Kashmiri wedding. They could keep the Registry Office and the church.

It was the goose-shooting season. We hardly ever got meat and we were going on a goose-shoot. Ramani borrowed an ancient twelve-gauge shotgun, a single-barrelled hammergun, and fourteen cartridges. We went over to the town and got a ride out to the goose lake on our friend's truck. We took up our position at the edge of the lake among some trees.

There were huge rafts of geese out on the water, thousands of them. The rich people were paddling around shooting them from shikaras. We were poor so we had to wait for something to fly past us. There were geese flying everywhere.

Ramani missed the first four geese that flew past, firing wildly in their general direction. I told him I was a champion shotgun-shot in my land – I was compared to him – and he willingly let me take the gun. I think he was a bit scared of it.

A big goose flew past about forty yards away and I dropped it. The Chella ran across to retrieve it.

"Allah be praised!" said Ramani. "A whole goose! We can give to Hasan. His eyes are bad to shoot the goose now."

"Yeah, sure," I said.

Another goose flew right over our heads. I shot it and it fell among some hashish-bushes at the edge of the lake. The Chella ran to retrieve it.

"Allah be praised!" cried Ramani. "We can give that one to old Kora. Her husband gone in the mud."

"Sure, Ramani."

We got eight geese before we ran out of cartridges. We gave away seven of them and ate one ourselves.

The Chella and I had a little trick of flicking the best bits of food to the other one's side of the bowl as though by accident. Then you'd find it had been accidently flicked back again. I usually ended up biting the bit of meat in half and making him take his share, which he would bite in half and offer me the rest, which I would refuse, whereupon he would drop it back into the bowl, swearing he couldn't eat any more or he was going to explode, so I'd go to offer it to the baby and he'd grab it and pop it into his mouth. *We* came first with the Chella. Me first, him next.

There was hardly enough meat on that goose to give us all a proper taste of it. We'd kept the smallest one for ourselves. Ramani explained that we would always have the geese we'd given away. We only lose the one we keep for ourselves. Hungry as we were for meat, I had to love the man. We all did. There was no arguing with him, it was right there in the Koran, in the words of Muhammed Himself.

We hardly ever had meat. Once or twice a month a hunk of mutton, mostly fat, but you could distinctly taste mutton. I couldn't tell us about the meat I used to have access to in my land. They wouldn't have been able to imagine it, but I resented those people in New Zealand and other places who wasted so much meat and other food when we didn't have enough to keep our teeth in our heads.

It's only as I write this that I realise how deeply into that family I was being drawn. Easy-led, I guess.

CHAPTER EIGHT

The part of my mind I always keep ajar was sending smoke signals about losing contact altogether with the outside world. (The most thing remind me my family the Chella talking like my talk.) I had a think about it and decided to bring my wife and the boys to Kashmir.

"You thinking funny today, Saab," said the Chella.

I shook him away with my head and went to find Ramani.

"I miss my wife and sons here," I told him.

"We miss them," he almost wept. "Send them walla yourd (come here)!"

The Chella, Ramani, Gulam, Abdul and I went over to the town in the big shikara and all crowded into the phone compartment at the post office and I rang Kevin in London to send the Saab's wife and sons, walla yourd.

My wife had taken off, kids and all, with another bloke and nobody knew where they were. Someone thought they were on a yacht around the Canary Islands or somewhere.

Suddenly I was in trouble again. This time it was my four Kashmiri brothers crowded into a phone-booth with me, waiting for me to say when the rest of our family was arriving. Talk about stuck for words! I mucked about with the phone.

"She's not there," I told them.

"We come back here tomorrow," said Ramani. He knew something was wrong.

"Sure, we'll do it that way," I said.

Back on our island I was having a big think. I'd lost my wife and the boys. She had all our money, I'd given Ramani most of what I had for our rice, expecting to be able to send to her for more. The only way I could go on living here was by writing, and there was no way I could write and publish a book in time to save being a burden on us. It was getting into winter and the road out of here could be closed for months by ice and snow.

I had to leave here, soon, and I didn't like it. I wasn't even sure I could handle it out there any more, but we just couldn't feed us all and I was the only one who could go. The others were going to struggle to get through the winter as it was. The tourist season had been disrupted by the riots and the rice we were getting was no good.

Some say that Kashmiri rice is the best in the world. It's the best I've eaten. They irrigate by hand and work up the ground with oxen and plant each plant and look after it and harvest it and process it, all by hand. The Americans, in India had developed a strain of rice with twice the size of grain and capable of producing two crops a year. They irrigated with pumps and used tractors and machinery to plant and harvest and process it. But there was nothing in it. You had to eat twice as much and it still wasn't enough. The Indians knew this and they'd started taking our good Kashmiri rice and giving us their empty rice instead of it. They were starving us.

I noticed that the Chella wasn't there and then I heard crying in the houseboat. I hadn't been in there for weeks. That was for the tourists. The Chella was in one of the rooms crying his heart out. Big wracking sobs. I picked him up off the floor and held him.

"What?" I said.

"Oh Saab, we're so sad today!" he sobbed.

Like a cat you suddenly notice is sitting on your lap I realised that the Chella was deeper into me than I'd believed. Trapped again. This time by a big heart with a young boy wrapped around it. I'd been abruptly cut off from everyone I loved. I wished it was yesterday.

That night I explained the whole situation to us, and we were very sad. Gulam wanted to go and find the man who'd run away with The Saab's wife and sons and put him in the mud.

I always seemed to come undone on islands. Shipwrecked on Three Isles, marooned on Lizard Island, and now I was separated from everything I cared about on Goosani Island.

I left Kashmir a week later. I got Gulam a pass by telling them he was working for me and took him on the back of the bike. I can't describe what it was like leaving there. I remember the Chella sobbing himself to sleep in my arms.

I had to concentrate to remember how to operate the bike. I was in a quite different state from when I rode in here. I was actually nervous of the thing, I didn't like it any more. My nerves came right the further we went, and Gulam's got worse. He'd never been out of Kashmir before, or on a motorbike. We came off a couple of times, once on ice in a black mile-long tunnel with a string of army trucks bearing down on us, which didn't help maKers, and the size and traffic of New Delhi is a bit overwhelming for anyone. As well as that Gulam was scared of the people, they were Hindus, he reckoned, and always persecuted us Moslems. We got a room at the Bright Hotel and had toast and tea sent up to us.

To prepare Gulam for the hassles of getting around the world I took him into a bank and showed him how to change most of our money into Traveller's Cheques, then I sent him on his own to change some of it back into rupees at another bank, warning him not to try changing any money on the street. He wanted me to go with him in case he did it wrong, but I made him go on his own. And he came back to the hotel in a state of tears and shock about an hour later. He'd been ripped-off for nearly all our money. He took me and showed me how it had happened.

Two and a half streets from our hotel there was a shop with a peeling BANK OF INDIA sign across the front of it, probably a genuine branch of the bank at one time. The shop was empty, with a counter and a grille. A middle-aged Indian in a suit had come to the counter and taken Gulam's Traveller's Cheques, advised him to sign a few extra (nearly all of them) because the exchange-rate had just turned favourable to the dollar, and then went out'the back and through a door that opened onto the junction of three teeming streets.

The shop was completely bare, not even a scrap of paper anywhere, but Gulam wouldn't have known that there was anything unusual about that. He still thought the bank was genuine and that was how all Hindus treated all Muslims. They wouldn't have done that if The Saab was there!

I got him back to the hotel and tried to make him know that it wasn't his fault, and the Indians didn't know he was a Kashmiri or a Muslim. He looked at me with stricken eyes and with both hands fiercely gripping my forearm and hissed, "Don't let them put me in the mud, Saab!"

I wasn't getting through to him. He knew I was saying the truth but his deep-rooted fear of Hindus wouldn't let him believe it. I ordered tea and toast and did my best to try and keep Gulam from drifting into his nightmare. That night I was half-woken a few times by him praying. He was saying 'The Saab' in his prayers, bless him.

Gulam had set out to see the world – London, Paris, New York, and I'd set out for New Zealand. We had just over a hundred rupees, a battered BMW motorbike, and a chronic case of religious and cultural shock on our hands.

The next day Gulam wouldn't come out of the hotel room because he was afraid the Hindus were going to knife him. He was a bit calmer by the time we'd had tea and toast, and I left

148

him there and went down to the government buildings, where I learned that I not only couldn't sell the bike in India, I had to surrender it unconditionally to the Indian Government before they'd clear my passport to leave the country.

By the time I got back to the hotel Gulam was losing it completely. The hotel management was most uncomfortable about his attitude towards them. They were Hindus, I could feel his fear of them. They thought we were both mad and I couldn't blame them. I made them go away and bring tea and toast, and I was just getting Gulam settled down when there was a loud knock on the door that frightened him into a corner behind a closet thing.

While I'd been waiting to get in to see someone about seeing someone about my bike, it attracted the attention of two Indian blokes, Arun and Vijay, and we'd got talking. They were academic types and when I told them I was a writer they invited me up to the university for a meal with Vijay's mother, who was a lecturer in English there.

"Are you Hindus?" I asked them.

"Why, yes," said Arun. "Why do you ask?"

I couldn't very well up and tell them that I had a half-crazy Kashmiri Muslim brother snookered in a hotel room across town who would have died of terror on the way to having a meal with them.

"Are there any Muslims around here?" I asked.

"Of course," said Vijay. "There are people of all religions in Delhi."

"Do you know any of them?" I asked.

They looked at each other. They didn't.

"They don't usually associate with us heathens," laughed Arun.

149

I excused myself from their invitation for a meal with Vijay's Hindu mother, exchanged names and addresses with my new Hindu friends and hurried back to my Muslim brother. And it was Arun knocking on our door to invite me to come and join them at a coffee-house. I got directions and said I'd meet them soon. Then I had to get Gulam out from his corner and settled down praying before I could leave him .

I met Arun, Vijay, Vijay's sister Manju, and two other people at a noisy coffee-house not far from the railway station. I didn't waste much time, I dragged Vijay and Arun aside and told them as much as necessary about the predicament I was in with Gulam. I needed help, even Hindu help. Neither of them could believe how scared of Hindus Gulam was until they met him. Between us we got him along to the station and onto a train to Jammu, where he could get a ride on a truck back to Kashmir. We embraced and parted on the crowded platform. O my Brother Gulam! That's what it's like out here though, mate.

The next couple of days were a bit depressing. I was having trouble surrendering my bike to the government. I could have hurried things up if I'd been able to pay various people bribes, but I was almost out of money. I couldn't even buy enough gas to get me back to Kashmir. And to make matters more complicated Vijay's sister, Manju, had fallen in love with me. It was in her horoscope. She came to my hotel room unchaperoned, which was unheard of. I told her I was already married, it made no difference. She didn't care how many other wives I had. Those Indians live their lives by their horoscopes. I had to try to avoid her.

I was having trouble handling all this. I'd had it. I went to the New Zealand embassy and asked to be repatriated. They took my particulars and then told me the best they could do was advance me the equivalent of forty dollars. I thanked them and left.

Back at the Bright Hotel they were hassling me for three hundred-odd rupees. I had ten. They wouldn't even bring me tea and toast any more. I sat on the bunk in the room wanting to be back in Kashmir with the others. It was just after Christmas in New Zealand and everyone I knew would be away on holiday and everything shut. The Commonwealth Games were on in Christchurch, I'd learned, and that wouldn't make it any easier to get there. There was a good chance I could get the bike freed off my passport the next day. It had become a burden. I decided to try and walk and hitch back home to Kashmir. One of the hotel Indians knocked on the door.

"You pay now," he called out.

"Tomorrow!" I called back. "Bring tea and toast."

"No tea and toast. Tomorrow we get the police," he called, and he went away.

Just after that the New Zealand Embassy Mercedes pulled up and two blokes got out. One of them paid my bill and the other came up and got me, and before I knew it I was sitting at the embassy table with about ten other people, eating pheasant and baked potato and green peas and red wine.

The commissioner, Grahame, was a real good bloke, more than helpful. He had them send a message on their satellite system to a friend of mine in Auckland, asking him to send me an air ticket to New Zealand and some money. I knew I should have been very grateful but I just wanted to get out of there. The lights were too bright, the food was too rich, the laughter was too loud and the people were over-dressed and flashy. I knew that there was nothing wrong with them, I was seeing them as a Kashmiri sees us. Grahame was trying to make some

151

arrangements with me but they weren't sinking in. I asked to be excused and they got a bloke to run me back to the hotel, where I was treated like royalty. I'd brought great prestige on the place. As much toast and tea as I wanted!

I was going back to New Zealand and didn't know how I was going to handle it. I would have preferred to return to Kashmir. The price of my air-fare to New Zea,land would probably keep us in rice right through the winter. I was confused. The people who were helping me were also telling me what I needed to do and I couldn't tell if it was the right thing or not.

The next morning the embassy car arrived to pick me up. The hotel management threw themselves in my path, offering hitherto-unmentioned services. I'd hinted to them that I was on secret Government business. Grahame had lent me the embassy accountant who certainly knew his Indians. He took us to the bank of India and showed them that they'd been authorised to issue me with five hundred dollars' worth of American Express travellers cheques. Then we went to British Airways and picked up my ticket and put me on a waiting list for a flight to New Zealand. After that we went round and surrendered my bike unconditionally to the Indian government and freed my passport. He knew his stuff, that accountant.

I'd been invited to have dinner at the embassy but I ate instead with my Indian friends, Vijay and Arun and some of their family, the beautiful Manju gazing disconcertingly at me all evening. She took a fancy to an embroidered Kashmiri scarf I had, so I gave it to her and in return she pressed on me an old woven silver bracelet. This turned out to be a not-very-good idea, it gave Manju hope. I avoided her all over Delhi, not always successfully. It's quite amazing how someone can find you in all those teeming millions of people. I even considered changing my hotel, but the situation wasn't to last long.

A few days later, at five o'clock in the morning, out of sixty people on the waiting list I was the only one to turn up and there was a spare seat on a plane to Bangkok, where I fluked a ride on an empty Japanese plane to Sydney, where I fluked another seat on a TWA plane to Auckland.

CHAPTER NINE

My trip overseas had had quite an effect on me. I'd left New Zealand a thirteen-and-a-half-stone extrovert, game for anything, with a wife and two sons, four new suitcases of luggage and plenty of money. Two years later I arrived back alone with about ten pounds of stuff in my saddlebags, owing money and under ten stone in weight. A gaunt, shy stranger with a queer accent and the Chella throwing tantrums in my soul. Some of my friends asked me straight-out if I was on drugs.

I needed some time to get my act together. I borrowed some more money and bought an old Austin van and a guitar and some stationery. I stuck a bunk in the van and drove south. The first time I actually relaxed since leaving our island on Dal Lake three weeks before was when I was parked-up at Franz Joseph Glacier with a decent fire going and a pair of cheeky keas trying to divert my attention from the Chella fretting and arguing about me leaving him behind. I had the absurd notion that I'd come to this mountainous place because he would feel more at home there.

The Chella thing is a bit of a mystery to me. I've never been over-attached to other people and wouldn't have guessed that anything like that would happen to me. It's faded over the years and doesn't bother me at all these days, though I can still tell you how old the Chella is without thinking. As I write this he's twenty-six. I've never contacted my Kashmiri friends since I left there and yet I feel as though I've never been out of touch with them.

I drove around the South Island for a couple of weeks, getting back into being a Kiwi again, deliberately doing things like putting butter on my bread and milk in my tea, wearing thick clothes and shoes and socks, correcting my Kashmiri lingo and generally hurrying myself back into Kiwi life. And it wasn't easy.

I'd become adjusted to living among people who never knew what it was like to have more in your bowl than you could eat. Here it was worse than I remembered it. The people, my people, were so knee-deep in material stuff that they couldn't keep track of it all, and everyone seemed to be blindly striving for more. I'd thank someone for a meal that would have been a banquet where I'd come from, and they'd say it should have been better only they had no vinegar for the salad-dressing. Or I'd remark how nice someone's house was and they'd apologise that some of the furniture was getting old. If I commented how nice someone's car looked they'd say the new model was even better, disc-brakes and power steering! It cost me more than a bag of rice was worth to get a puncture fixed. In Kashmir they struggle with too little, here the struggle is with too much. Half of what most of us have is twice as much as we need, and twice what they've got is half what they need.

I drifted around trying to get used to all this, and then one day I dropped a hitch-hiker off at the Greymouth Youth Hostel and saw the word BAHAI written across the back of a car parked there, and it hit me like a ton of bricks. Wouldn't go out of my head.

By this time the spiritual strand of my rope was getting a bit frayed on it. When I was very young I realised that all adults believed that all children needed saving, especially me. When I was about four a man who was visiting my grandmother's house sprinkled some water on my hair out of a small bottle and begged the Lord to forgive me in strange muttering language. I must have done something pretty wicked because I needed a lot of forgiving. It must have worked all right

156

because I immediately lost all memory of what it was I needed forgiving for. This left me in danger of unknowingly doing the same things again and needing more of that forgiving, so I wasn't terribly impressed.

There was Sunday School and the Holy Ghost and not going to heaven if you did wrong things. Then when I was about nine an aunt took me to a Christian Revival meeting in a hall in Khyber Pass Road. There were a lot of them happening around then. We were going to be saved by a wonderful man who'd been touched by God. The hall was full of strange-looking people, all standing up because there were no seats.

All you could hear for a while was shuffling and coughing, and then this man in a suit came on the stage and told us that everyone in the hall was wicked and evil and destined to burn in the fires of hell and damnation for all eternity. There were blasphemers amongst us! There were hypocrites! And adulterers! Heretics! We were things called transgressors! No wonder we looked a bit strange.

I stood there wondering if the lady in front of me was a blasphemer or an adulterer, while the man who'd been touched by God walked around on the stage telling us how utterly doomed and hopeless we all were. But, he said, there was one way out. We could go down on our knees and beg the Lord for forgiveness and salvation.

"Go down onto your knees for the Lord!" he shouted.

And all of a sudden there were people going down on their knees around the hall, praying and muttering and calling out, Hallelujah!, while the man on the stage called out for everyone to open their wretched hearts and let the Lord in to save them. Pretty soon nearly all the people were on their knees, including my aunt, all praying for that forgiveness. There were only a few of us left standing up in the whole hall.

I waited for it to happen to me. I could hear the man who'd been touched by God telling me to let the Lord into my heart, I could even see the spit from his words against the light, but I was still waiting when he began to tell everyone to give, give, give for the Lord! Suddenly there were men in suits going along the rows of kneeling people with small galvanised buckets, collecting money and thanking each brother and sister. It seemed that the Lord only wanted donations from those who'd been saved because the man didn't even look at me as he reached past me to take my aunt's two half-crowns.

That man did save me in a way. He saved me from having to endure any more embarrassment by thanking everyone and abruptly leaving the stage as soon as all the money was collected. I almost ran out of there and waited for my aunt at the bus stop. If that was how you got saved, I was indeed lost. My aunt was a bit disapproving of me not accepting the Lord into my heart when I had the chance, but she reassured me that He would undoubtedly touch me in His own good time. Listening to her description of that meeting later it seemed to me that we'd been to different meetings.

I continued to resist all efforts to save me and although my mother was always praying for me I left home and went out into the world quite unforgiven. Over the years I ran into all sorts of people who reckoned they had The Answer, and I gave them all a go, or nearly all of them. Some things people get into are right off the wall as far as I'm concerned.

I flicked through Tarot readings, the I Ching, astrology, ouija-boards, hypnotism and microbiotics. I checked them out as I ran into them and couldn't believe that any of them was the answer. Not for me, anyway.

When I was in Auckland I ran into this bloke who was right into Scientology, reckoned it was the answer. I read some of the literature he gave me and agreed to visit their headquarters, where a bloke sat me in a booth holding a lie detector and asked me questions about my family and myself.

When you're swinging off the end of a lie-detector there's only one way to go. I answered all the bloke's questions as honestly as I could, and came out of there with a certificate saying that I was Grade O Communications Release. My skepticism was unscathed. It wasn't the answer I was looking for.

I ran into a talking-in-tongues-interpreter and let him talk me into going to one of their meetings. The friends were scattered thinly about the hall. The preacher started praying fervently and soon he became incoherent. Then people around the hall started calling out and raving in a most embarrassing manner. I got up and walked out of there. If that was where it was at, I'd missed out on it forever.

At one stage there was a belief afoot that psychology held the answers. I read Freud and Jung and a few other psychology books, and came away with an abiding suspicion of that science.

There were always plenty of places to look for the answer. Jehovah's Witness, Seventh Day, Mormon, Gihal Gibran, Faith Healing, Transcendental Meditation, Maharajahs in Mercedes Benz cars and born-again Christians.

"Get yourself baptised," they said.

"No," I said.

"Primal Scream Therapy?"

"No, I don't think so."

Then there was my journey to find The Answer in India, enough has been said about that. And now there was this Bali Hai thing to be investigated and chucked on the heap with the rest of them. What the hell, I had nothing else to do anyway. It was a change to have a purpose in life, even if it was something as flimsy as investigating a word.

One of my friends was a Bahai. I found her in Auckland and borrowed some books from her and parked up in the Parnell Rose Gardens and started reading. And one of the first things I ran into was that the Bahai Faith was dedicated to the abolishment of extremes of poverty and wealth. That rocked me, this was going to take a bit of looking-into.

The Bahai writings are voluminous, and I soaked them up, reading day and night. I had to buy candles because I was flattening the battery in the van. The weeks went by. I got to know the rosegardeners and always had a rose or two in the van. The police on patrol at night would drop by for a brew of tea and a yarn. As soon as they were gone I'd get back into reading. I was finding answers to questions I'd been asking all my life.

It made sense to me. Every few hundred years a new Prophet of God is sent among men to repeat the spiritual teachings of all the previous Prophets and bring new social laws to bring us into the next age, like stages of education. And the Bahai Prophet has given us more than a hundred volumes in his own handwriting, sticking His neck out on every subject. If there were any flaws in His teachings they should be easy enough to find.

I didn't find any. The weeks turned into months. I got two unexpected royalty-payments and paid off the money I owed, which was a great relief. I was getting bewildered with all the stuff I was absorbing. I took off south to have a few adventures and clear my head, driving around with nowhere in particular to go, just enjoying the travel and the people I met. Doodling with adventure.

I'd brought two young blokes over to Turangi from near Wairoa and camped in a side road among the broom and scrub and did a bit of reading. Early next morning I was trundling along south and saw this bloke walking along. He looked like a recycled hippy, long hair, leather jacket with strips hanging off it, beads and bracelet. He had a bedroll on a strap over his shoulder and a leather bag on one hip. I stopped and asked him if he needed a lift. He said he was going to the desert so I told him to hop in, it was a few miles up ahead of us.

He was American or Canadian, by his accent, late teens – early twenties. He'd arrived in New Zealand a week before and he was going to the desert. He said his name was Pat. We drove along in silence, with Pat examining everything in the van as though he'd never been in one before, until we came to the desert part of the road. It was winter and there were patches of snow around. Pat made me stop so he could walk in the snow and pick up handfuls and crush it and taste it. He'd never seen snow close up before, he lived in a place where it never happened. He began to remind me of Gulam.

We drove on and Pat found a booklet in the shelf under the dash and began to read it. It was a compilation of Bahai writings on the oneness of all the human tribes and races. I don't think he even looked up as we passed through Waiouru. We were coming into Taihape when he looked round him and said,

"Where do you get this writing?"

"It's Bahai," I told him. "I'm looking into it."

"Where's the desert?" he said.

"Back there where that snow was," I told him.

"That's the desert?"

"The only official one. If you want real desert you'll have to go to Australia."

"I have to go back," he said.

I stopped the van.

"You sure?" I asked him.

"I'll walk," he said.

"I'll take you," I said and we turned back, and on the way Pat came out with this strange story.

His real name was Patatonga or something, and he was the chief's son of a small tribe of desert Indians. He'd been picked by his grandfather to fulfill a prophecy that had been handed down through the generations. When the tribe reached a stage of utter hopelessness they were to send someone of noble lineage to a green land under the South Star to find the spirit of one of their ancestors, who would show them the path out of the wilderness to a world of peace and happiness. Pat had duly arrived in Auckland and (Gulam again!) got a bit freaked-out by it all. He'd been told that if he couldn't find his ancestor he was to go into the desert and wait. He'd walked nearly all the way from Auckland because he was on the wrong side of the road half the time and he never asked for lifts. His appearance was against him a bit as well. And now he'd run into me and a Bahai book on the Oneness of Mankind on the Desert Road in a green land under the South Star. He was shining with excitement. Looked like a different bloke.

Probably because of my recent experiences in Kashmir, I'm afraid I panicked.

"Look here mate, I told him. "I'm no one's bloody ancestor. I'm just giving you a lift."

"No," he said, holding up the booklet he'd been hanging onto all the time. "It's this. These are the words my grandfather said would make me know their own truth."

"I hope you know what you're doing."

"Isn't this the truth?" he said, holding the booklet out towards me.

"I wouldn't like to put you crook, mate," I said. "I'm still looking into it myself."

"What more is there to find?" he said.

We stopped by Pat's patch of snow and had tea and toast. He was convinced that he'd found what he'd come to find, and I couldn't convincingly disagree with him. I gave him four Bahai books and left him at a hut I knew of at the foot of the Kaimanawa Range. He wanted to be alone with what he'd found. So did I. The man had shaken me. I'd been absorbing the Bahai writings for months, the best part of a year, and this bloke had seen the simple truth of it in a pamphlet out of someone's glovebox.

I've heard that there are now a number of Bahai groups among the American Indian tribes, and I wonder if Pat and I meeting on the Desert Road that day had anything to do with that. It had a fair bit to do with me. I returned to Auckland and registered myself as a Bahai, and I've been one ever since.

It's exciting to know that this knowledge is there to be found by anyone who can read. Anyone who investigates for themselves with an open mind the events that began two hours and thirteen minutes after sunset on May the twenty-second, eighteen forty-four in Shiraz in Persia, will realise that Bahai holds the solutions to all the problems that beset humanity in this day.

That's a pretty extravagant claim, and in sixteen years of living as a Bahai as best I can, everything I've seen confirms it to be the truth.

I got an English translation of the Koran and read the verses that had so inspired us in Kashmir. I also read the Bible and the Bhagvad Gita. There's only one story of humanity, and for me it all comes together in the Bahai writings.

I'd been getting letters from Manju. Long ones, all pointing out what a terrific wife she'd make. And, talking of wives, around this time a friend who'd just come from England said I ought to go and get my kids, who were living in a cottage, in

163

Sussex. My wife's boyfriend had been jailed in Morocco for smuggling. She'd made it back to England with the boys and they were having a tough time of it. She was in trouble over some missing diamonds. I borrowed again and flew to England and found them. They'd been broke for a fair while and had sold everything they could. I brought them back to New Zealand.

I'd been curious to see what would happen between me and my wife. Nothing did, our paths were well and truly parted. I got them into a flat in Auckland and left them to it. The next time I saw her she had another bloke. Thanks mate.

Brother Bill and Brother Colin were making solar panels at Henderson, and I camped in one of their sheds and gave them a hand for a few months. Bill was the first president of the NZ Solar Manufacturers Association.

During this time I rebuilt an old BSA 500 single-banger motorbike and did a bit of cruising around the north on it. They're a sensation to ride after being used to the modern bikes. In my spare time I built a whare on a mate's place in the Waitakeres. Then I swapped the bike for a 1941 V8 truck, which I did up and exchanged for a 1930 Model A Ford, which I rebuilt. Must have been in a reconstructive frame of mind around then.

The Model A was a car cut down into a small truck with a canvas canopy on the back. When I got it going right I threw a bit of gear into it and hit the road again. I'd been around there for long enough.

Whenever I move on and have to start up on the road again I get what I privately call my kick-off kit. Teabags, a tin of condensed milk, a large tin of peaches and a tin of cream. Cut the tops out of the peach and cream tins and eat the contents. Fold the top of the peach tin into a band and bend it into a handle and wire it onto the cream tin. That's me mug. Then I put a wire handle on the peach tin and that's me billy. Then I carve myself a spoon out of a piece of wood, preferably a splinter off a totara post, and I'm all set up for that best of all drinks, a brew of tea.

Anyway – I was in Greymouth, almost broke, when I met up with Robyn. Didn't even know she was in the South Island, she came from Gisborne. I'd noticed this fascinating looking girl at Bahai gatherings and we'd never seen enough of one another. I ran into one of the Bahais in the street in Greymouth and she told me that they were having a birthday party for Robyn at their house that night.

I went, and about an hour after I arrived we loaded Robyn's trailbike and gear onto the Model-A and took off down State Highway Six on an adventure that was to last for twelve years. Robyn was just twenty-one and I was forty-three.

CHAPTER TEN

Our first camp was an empty farmhouse we rented, out from Hokitika. We furnished it out of the Hokitika dump. It's always amazed me what people chuck out. Good stuff with years of use left in it, thrown on the dump to make way for a newer model. Seems pretty wasteful to me. I've written two books about rubbish-tip people. Must be a bit of a scavenger myself.

We bought some second-hand traps and trapped the swamps and roadsides to get some money. After a few weeks we moved south and camped up Rough Creek in the Karangarua, sleeping in the Model-A and cooking over an open fire. We ran trap-lines up and down the ridges and spurs of the Alps and got enough skins to keep us going. It was real cold and the only way we could keep warm at night was to heat up a decent-sized rock in the fire and wrap a sack around it and put it in our bed.

Robyn was a good bushman from the start. In no time she was running her own line of traps and getting about as many skins as me.

The first time I realised that Robyn had real guts was when we'd laid a poison-line one day up on a high ridge upstream from our camp and tried to drop over into the head of Rough Creek and follow it down to the camp. We made it to within three hundred feet or so of the creek and found that the face we were on curved over into a sheer drop onto boulders. Rough Creek was well named. Then I pulled the whole root system of a small tree out of the cliff-face and we couldn't get back up the way we'd come. We had to sidle across rotten crumbling rock to a finger-ridge with a bit of shrubbery to cling to.

By guiding every foot and hand-hold I got us up onto the crest of the ridge again. It was too late to make it back to our camp the way we'd come, or any other way for that matter. We could look down into Rough Creek and see the Model-A and the fireplace and the stuff hanging on the trees, two and a half thousand feet below us, but it might as well have been a hundred miles away, there was less than an hour's daylight left. It was a night out in the bush for us.

We found where a tree had come down and while I built up a reasonable sort of fire against the trunk with shattered branches and gathered all the wood around Robyn sidled round into a creek-head and brought back a gumbootfull of water. Yuck – but, with that and an apple from the possum-lure bag we lasted out a freezing night.

The longest nights I've known are the ones I've spent caught out in the bush, they're never comfortable, but that one was the least uncomfortable. Robyn and I could spend hours just talking.

Next morning we back-tracked on our poison-line and took the skins. There were more than eighty of them and we arrived back at our camp in the afternoon weak from exhaustion and hunger. And not a word of complaint from Robyn. I knew then that she was a Good Keen Woman.

When the whitebait season started we moved further south and took a stand at the mouth of the Black River, nine miles in from the road down a swampy track that was often impassable. We parked the Model-A out at the road and didn't see it again for three months. We had the use of a small hut, a luxury after having just spent the winter virtually in the open.

The mouth of the Black River is a pretty place, with a hedge of golden kowhai trees along one bank, filled with tui and native pigeons. The river emerged into the sea at one end of a three-mile beach, which was all ours any time we wanted.

Our stand was the front one, nearest the sea, but that didn't mean we were going to get any more whitebait than any of the other four stands on the river that year. We built a small jetty from the bank out into the river, with posts and timber chain-sawed out of the bush, which grew right to the edge of the water. Then we made wire-mesh screens and nets to fit between the piles of the jetty.

We'd put our nets and screens in and sit on the stand, watching for shoals of whitebait coming up the river. It was quite often possible to drive a shoal of bait into your net by plonking a stone beyond them. Another trick, I think frowned upon by rangers, was to tack a silver tin-lid onto a long pole and flash it out in the river to chase whitebait towards your nets. We were getting as much bait as any of the others, no big runs but a steady trickle with most tides.

Some whitebaiters who had a big hut half a mile up the river took out our tins of bait and brought in our supplies on their tractor. All Robyn and I had to do was fish and swim and lay round in the sun eating cold pigeon sandwiches and drinking tea. Lazy happy days, after crawling up and down the sides of the Alps all winter.

One of the few people we saw that season was an old possum trapper called Dodge, named, he reckoned, after a car his old man had when he was born. I'd known Dodge when I was culling in the North Island. He was like a bit of flotsam left over from a previous generation. He'd been trapping possums all his life and in some respects he'd failed to keep up with modern trends. The Department of Conservation people would have been horrified to see Dodge casually drive his slasher halfway through a sapling and lever the split open to hang a possum in by the tail.

Dodge thought nothing of dropping a big rimu or kahikatea

169

tree across a creek or swamp on his trapline to save getting his feet wet or having to walk a few extra yards. He'd fell a matai to get a few rounds of firewood off the butt. He'd burn off a whole face of second-growth to make it easier to get through. I pointed out to him one day that he'd just ruined a tree, and he replied that he'd saved a few as well, so he was pretty square with the bush.

It rains a lot on the West Coast, and wet possum-skins are a fact of life. There's a lot of blowflies on the West Coast too, and maggots are a fact of life as well, and keeping his skins and the blowflies separated was a skill that Dodge never successfully mastered. He liked a yarn but when he met you at the doorway of his hut with his hair and jersey spotted with fly-eggs and a ceiling of steaming possum skins hanging from the roof behind him, only the brave or the reckless would have stayed for a brew with him.

We ended the whitebait season with enough money to get married and buy another motorbike and tour the North Island together. Then we went back south and picked up the Model-A and cruised over the Haast Pass to Otago. We'd heard about gold-panning but neither of us had ever done it. We'd decided to give it a go.

In Queenstown we bought two gold-pans and shovels and drove to a creek we got directed to a few miles out of town, and camped there. For two days we washed panfuls of creek gravel and not one speck of gold did we find, then an old bloke came past and showed us that we were digging in all the wrong places and how to pan properly. After that we started getting flakes and specks of gold in almost every pan of gravel.

It soon became obvious that we'd have to do more than pan for it if we were going to get enough gold to live on. The prices of the food in Queenstown were a shock. We had very little money left. We went into town and got some timber and made up two riffle-boxes, about a foot wide and four feet long. We could work the gravel much faster through those.

We'd become friendly with the run-holder and his family in the two weeks we'd been there and he gave us the combination to the lock of their gate so we could drive down the stream and camp on their property. The road, if you could call it that, followed the creek, and we camped on a grassy flat thirty crossings down from the gate. We had the place to ourselves.

By prospecting around the river beaches and banks we soon found where the best places for gold were. Some spots got replenished with each flood. We worked out that we were putting two and a half thousand shovelfuls of gravel through the riffle-boxes to get an ounce of gold. At a hundred and sixty dollars we weren't going to get rich in any hurry.

We lived on that river-flat for five months, eating mostly toast and rabbit, and when the winter came our friends who owned the station invited us to move into a ghost-town, a thousand feet or so above the creek we were camped in. The creekbed freezes up in the winter and the road is impassable. The only other way in and out was over the Moonlight Trail, two and a half hours to Arthur's Point. We left the Model-A out there and moved into the old library at Seffertown, named after a Russian family who'd lived there years before.

The room was about ten feet by eight, with a big stone fireplace in the back wall. We were warmer in there than the people out in town with big houses and small fires. We cleaned up the old town, nine buildings were still usable. Trapped possums all winter and when summer came we borrowed three horses off a friend who wasn't using them, one each to ride and one for a packhorse, and did a bit of work on the trail and mostly went in and out that way. We'd done well on skins and we still had a couple of ounces of gold from last summer, so we bought an old wheel-tractor with a front-end loader on it and had a big steel box made, with three layers of expandite on carpet for riffles. We'd set it up and dam the creek till we had the right amount of water running through it. I'd drop the buckets of gravel into the box and Robyn would keep the big stones moving with a garden hoe and watch for nuggets.

We started getting a third to half an ounce of gold in a three- or four-hour working day. Flakes and small nuggets mostly. It was all the mining we needed to do. The rest of the time we rode around exploring the Moonlight Valley and the country around it. Tussock and rock, with patches of beech bush. Brown-paper country. We were happy, neither of us needed, or particularly wanted, anyone else around.

That summer we cut half an acre of hay with an old scythe and stacked it in one of the huts for winter feed for our horses. We trapped skins again through the winter and when the summer came round we resumed our mining operation. We were getting good at it. We took out a Prospecting Licence and then a Mining Licence on about a mile of our creek. We were official gold-miners.

Then the price of gold went up, almost overnight, from a hundred and forty, to eight hundred dollars an ounce, and the whole gold-mining scene was suddenly changed. People are funny about gold. There was a lot of greed and argument. Areas that had been not worth doing were now valuable. No one would buy any gold in case the price came down, which it did. We ended up with more than a pound of gold in a jar and we couldn't sell it.

We both realised that we'd had enough of this place at the same time. Within a week we'd swapped the Model-A for a Volkswagen Combie and fitted it out to live in. We gave the claim and tractor and other gear to our friends and by the time we were a hundred Ks up the highway we could hardly remember what it had been like back there. Gold mining was one of the most enjoyable things I've ever done for a living, but two and a half years of it was enough for us to be going on with.

We headed north up the West Coast. It had been raining all day and night and the van leaked in a couple of places, so when it cleared up we stopped in a rest area beside the Buller River to dry some of our gear out. While Robyn draped our blankets and stuff over some low bushes I grabbed a gold-pan and went over to the river. It was a bit flooded. I dug out a pan-full of gravel with the edge of the pan at the water's edge and roughly panned it out. There were four large flakes of gold and thirty-five specks. I took the pan across and showed it to Robyn.

"Where did you get that?" she said.

"At the edge of the river just over there," I told her. "One panful."

We looked at each other for a few seconds and then I threw the gold out of the pan and put it back under the bunk. It could be used for washing-up in after this.

We drifted to the far north and camped in a disused quarry for two or three weeks while I wrote a book. Got the title off a sign up there, *Puha Road*. We took it down to Auckland and got it printed and distributed. Robyn did most of the office-type work connected with it. It sold quite well and while we had some money we decided to have a spell in the tropics. We'd done it a bit cool the last few winters. We parked our van in Brother Colin's shed and flew up to the Cook Islands.

After a few weeks in Rarotonga we went up to Aitutaki and rented a hut on the back of the island beside the lagoon. We were struck by the similarities between the New Zealand Maoris and the Cook Islanders. There's no doubt they knew each other somewhere back down the line. We borrowed an outrigger canoe and fixed it up a bit and put a sail on it, loaded some supplies into it and sailed off across the lagoon to the farthest motu, Tapuaetahi, a distance of about seven miles. When we got there we found that Robyn, who was wearing shorts, was badly sunburnt on the tops of her legs.

This was a worry. It could be days, or even weeks, before we got a favorable wind to take us back to Aitutaki, and Robyn's legs were looking more serious all the time. She could hardly walk. Coconut juice was all we could think of.

Robyn was right into shinning up coconut trees and getting fresh nuts, but she could hardly even walk. I couldn't get up there, it's harder than it looks. I managed to drag a bunch of nuts down with a rope and we split them on a sharpened stick and scraped out the flesh and squeezed it through a cloth and applied it to Robyn's burns. It was almost miraculous how that fresh coconut cream fixed that sunburn. In two days she was as right as rain.

We built a small thatched hut on the island and swam and fished and speared and explored the reef and the neighboring islands. That was just about all there was to do there, and after a few weeks we could tell it was time to get going before we got bored with it.

In spite of us having kept to ourselves a bit, we'd made some really close friends among the Cook Islanders, and there were tears and flowers at the airport when we left. We returned to Auckland and camped in our van on an old poultry farm Brother Colin owned in Henderson.

I'd written a short book while we were in the Cook Islands and Robyn and I published it. *Shorty*, I called this one. It must be some sort of record for publishing, that book, three weeks from typescript to the bookshops. I wrote it in about ten days. It may be being made into a film. Probably a short one.

There's a lot of waiting around with publishing, and we camped down the back of a golf course and swung clubs from daylight till dark. Thirty-six holes was hardly enough for a day's golf. We played on many other courses and didn't improve much, despite me doing things like standing in the van headlights at ten o'clock at night, hitting balls up the dark fairway to practice a swing I'd found described in a book.

It couldn't last, there's no money in golf at our level. It all changed in one day. We didn't know it was Ladies Day at the golf course and Robyn got caught doing our washing in the women's changing-rooms. They let her know they took a very dim view of that sort of thing. It would have to be reported to The Committee. Then when we took our van in to get a Warrant of Fitness we found that the chassis was almost completely rusted through.

We'd already spent heaps on that van. The motor, the brakes, the wheel-bearings, the steering-box – we should have just about had a new waggon, and now the blasted thing was falling in half and we didn't have the money to get it fixed or swap it for something else. I was hacked off.

We drove along Lincoln Road in Henderson and I noticed this new ute parked outside a Toyota dealership. I pulled up and went over and had a look at it. It was a Toyota Hilux, four-wheel-drive one-ton ute. They had to be good. I went in and got the dealer to let me ring his head office in Wellington. The Marketing Manager came on the phone and I told him who I was.

"I've just seen your new four-by-four ute," I said. "I'll advertise them for you if you give me one."

"We've just been trying to think of someone to front our four-wheel-drive range," he said. "I think we might be able to do business."

We talked about it for a while. He seemed to be fair dinkum. I gave him an address where he could get in touch with me and went back out to the van.

"See that ute there," I said to Robyn.

"Yes."

"We'll be in a brand-new one in about a month."

It was the only time I'd ever offered to advertise anything. I'd had plenty of opportunities but I usually knocked them back in favour of trapping skins to get money. This was a bit different, this was wheels, good ones, brand-new ones. We were looking forward to that.

That same day we were talking to a bloke who distributed books for us, and in bounced Paddy O'Donnell, who informed me that I was going to work with him. He was the new breakfast announcer on Radio Pacific, which he and another couple of blokes had taken over and were trying to get running at a profit. I told him that Robyn and I always work together and he immediately offered her a job as well.

He actually had to come back twice before we accepted his offer. The money was good and we needed it, but it was the challenge of it that made us take him up on it, and a few days later I started sharing the Breakfast Session with Paddy, one of the brightest sparks I've ever met. They filmed me arriving at Radio Pacific in a Rolls Royce and cutting my way into the studio with a chainsaw. I think it was a TV news-item.

One of our friends had a dog that would snarl and growl something ferocious when you pulled on a rolled-up newspaper with him. We taped some snarling and growling and made out that Paddy and I had this dog called Scum in the studio with us.

176

Scum was a real bad egg. He ripped open the rubbish-bags, he wouldn't shut up when we were trying to read out important ads, he had to be kicked and slammed for threatening guests to the studio, he knocked things over, caused power cuts, scratched records, made people late, wouldn't let the station manager in the building, and generally got the blame for everything that went wrong round the station.

And the listeners loved him. They started sticking up for him. They knew Scum wasn't real, I told them he was an Irish Wolfhound crossed with an old pig-dog bitch my mate found in the Mamakus, but they liked joining in the fun. They wrote poems about him, one lady swore that her bitch had fallen in love with Scum from his voice over the radio. We held a Mongrel Dog Show at Western Springs and assembled the most fantastic array of hard-case dogs I ever saw in one place, including rabbit-packs and Ruatoria.

Things were evolving in the station. Robyn was learning how to operate the panel and handle the phone calls, and I was getting into talkback and liking it. I wangled my way into the early-morning shift, where there was more freedom. I'll never forget the night Robyn and I took over at midnight and ran the station till Paddy came on at five o'clock. We were the only ones in the building and we were pretty damn nervous. We picked out thirty-five records to play in case no one rang up.

It went all right, though, and it wasn't long before we were as good as any of them. Our good friend Paddy put me onto radio. Thanx mate!

I'll always prefer radio to television or filming work. Less concern with appearances. Disembodied voices from any distance or age, communicating with other voices. We called our programme *The Bush Telegraph*, and it didn't matter whether you had your teeth in or your strides on, you could always have your say on our programme, as long as you didn't rubbish any-one or anything. I refused to have anything to do with contro-versy or smut, there was plenty of that around already. And it was a good move. Our ratings became the best in Auckland at the time of day we were broadcasting. Just Robyn and me.

If you knew Robyn like I did you wouldn't have been able to keep a grin off your face, either, when you looked through that glass panel and saw her operating a radio station.

We worked various shifts, wherever we were needed, but we preferred the late-night stuff, the Graveyard Shift. It was more laid-back. Some of the subjects we got onto were a bit unorthodox. One night we talked excitedly for five hours about the different things that were kept on the back porch when we were kids, and the board was full of calls all night.

One old bloke came up with a rather ingenious alarm clock, guaranteed to wake you up at dawn any time of the year. All you have to do is open the fowl-run before you go to bed at night, and lay a trail of maize from the fowl-run gate to a tin tray under your bed.

Or we might decide to have a party, with the listeners singing and playing instruments over the phone, and me with a guitar in the studio. Some of the acts were such a crack-up that Robyn would have to stick on a record while we all settled down.

Button-accordions, recorders, fiddles, organs, old records, comb-and-paper, handsaws, many other acts – all got the dust blown off them on the Bush Telegraph. One bloke, I remem-ber, rang in and said he was going to play the darning needle for us. He held it between the finger and thumb of his right hand and sang, "Ouch, ouch, ouch, ouch; ouch, ouch, ouch!" to the tune of the National Anthem. Sometimes we didn't have time to read the ads we were supposed to, and Paddy would have to fit them into his Breakfast Session.

We had to take a week off to go to Wellington and film a television commercial for the Toyota Company. They put us into the flashest hotel either of us had ever been in. Our own private elevator, free drinks in your suite (looked free to us at the time), colour TV, huge bed, tons of hot water. And didn't Robyn lap it up. She ordered things from room service she didn't even want, just to have done it. She even got them to launder our bush-singlets and jeans because it was on the list of services available.

We shot the commercial in a block of cut-over bush near Wellington. It took three days. It was the first time I'd worked with Lloyd Scott (Scotty), and we hit it off straight away. He'd been doing acting and radio and television work for years and understood what we were supposed to be doing. He was easy to learn off. Heart in the right place, Scotty.

As soon as they finished filming, Robyn and I drove away in one of the utes we'd used in the ad. That was the deal; they gave us two thousand dollars and the free use of a ute for a year, then it was to be replaced with a new model. All we had to pay for was the gas we used. We were pleased with that deal. Wellington to Auckland on thirty bucks' worth of gas.

After all the years of grease and spanners and spares, micky-mousing and patching up old bombs and nursing them through their last few anxious miles, here we were in a brand-new diesel ute. I didn't even need to know what was under the bonnet. Mileage was nothing to us now!

We worked all week on the radio and drove around the country-side all weekend in the ute. Our programme was growing in popularity. One morning a bloke rang in and read us a poem he'd written and I told him I reckoned it was worth publishing. Within a week more than a hundred and fifty poems had been sent in. We were more or less obliged to do something with them.

I edited out about forty poems and got the listeners to send illustrations, Robyn handled the mail, a big job, and one of our friends at the station typed it all out for us. We got two thousand of them printed. A fifty-six-page collection of original poems, delightfully illustrated – all our own work!

Slim volumes of verse aren't famous for making money, but this one did. We only offered it to our listeners, by mail. Send us your money and we'll send you a book. It paid for itself in the first two weeks, and sold out altogether in four weeks. We let it go out of print. Robyn and I had risked five thousand dollars of our own money and the book made fourteen thousand. We gave some of it to listeners who were hard-up or in trouble.

I've picked this sample from the Bush Telegraph Collection of Original Verse because it was inspired by the atmosphere of the programme.

Bush Telegraph

I used to be a night-owl
Till Bush Telegraph came our way
Now I go to bed early
And wake up to the light of day.

My whole life has been altered
I'm getting more work done
The cheerfulness of the Programme
Is like the burst of the sun.

The response from the public is amazing
If Barry requests some ideas,
And memories from our childhood
Come pouring back over the years.

Politics grumbling or wingeing
Do we want them – we do not
Bush Telegraph unmistakably
Discourages them on the spot.

Butterflies, doggies, birds and the bees
Yarns with an animal theme
Memories whimsical, comic or pleasant
Fit into Bush Telegraph's theme.

I don't know what I did before
Barry's memoirs changed my life
They're an antidote for miseries
Unpleasantries, troubles and strife.

So after you've listened to the programme
And Barry has gone on his way –
Put on your loveliest smile
And have a wonderful day.

Eleanor.

Thanks, Eleanor.

CHAPTER ELEVEN

Some of the stuff our listeners were sending in or leaving at the desk for us was getting embarrassing. One bloke gave us an intricately-worked silver necklace over a hundred years old, with a hundred and fifty matched pearls hanging off it. Our flat was filling up with books and records and crockery and clocks – all manner of stuff, plus a whole lot of oddities the listeners had sent in for me to comment on. Like a four-foot bean, a Maori carving someone had found, a curiously-distorted swede. Anything unusual or interesting they wanted to share with the rest of us. Robyn was given most of it. She used to visit some of the listeners who couldn't get around and take them things they needed from other listeners who couldn't get around and she never came away without stuff being heaped on her, and yet they were usually people in need.

We got a lot of mail on that job, but there's one letter I'll never forget. It was from Jack, the bloke who rescued us from Three Isles when we were shipwrecked, and who I hadn't seen or heard of since I stood on the jetty at Cooktown and told him I didn't know how I was ever going to be able to thank him. His letter was to say that he couldn't thank me enough for the inspiration my programme had been to his mother, who was one of our listeners. She'd recently died after a long illness and the *Bush Telegraph* had been her main comfort and pleasure during her last few months. If that makes us square, Jack, it's the best deal I've ever had. Thank you mate, both times.

It started getting to us. We'd been working all sorts of hours for fourteen months and we'd never failed to turn up and we'd never been late. Not bad going for a couple of bush-rats like us. Irresponsible people take responsibility very seriously.

The off-air activities were becoming a bit overwhelming as

well. They started a Bush Telegraph Club, which was to meet at a listener's house, but by the time of the meeting so many people wanted to turn up we had to hold it in a hall. A bunch of us planned to take a ride on the Glenbrook steam train. We expected a dozen, maybe twenty people to turn up – more than twelve hundred registered for it.

We just couldn't keep it up. When we took this job Robyn and I made a deal that if one of us couldn't handle it we'd both chuck it in. There was no need to have made that deal, neither of us could take much more of it. Once again we'd both had enough at the san time. There was some consternation when we told them we were leaving next week.

Jim Henderson, an old friend and scribe, took over the hosting from me. He called it *Open Country*, and did a fine job for some years. Robyn and I gave away all the stuff we'd accumulated and took off for the bush in the ute. We rented a shack by a river near Opotiki in the Bay of Plenty, five dollars a week.

We trapped possums for a living and hunted and fished for food, and generally worked the dust of the city out of our lungs. After a few months we moved on and camped near Punakaiki on the West Coast, where I wrote a longish poem and dedicated it to our listeners on Radio Pacific. It was called *Mrs Windyflax and the Pungapeople*.

I sent the poem to Jim Henderson to read out to the listeners, and the station got so many requests for copies that they had to tell the people to send two dollars and a self-addressed envelope to me and Robyn. By this time we were camped in Golden Bay and there was only one photocopier we could find. It was in an office in Takaka and they didn't mind photocopying things for people, but we had to do hundreds of copies and it was five pages long. I began to wish I'd made it shorter. I don't know how many copies we had to churn out, but I remember that one day we put four hundred two-dollar notes in our bank. I'm afraid we were a bit of a nuisance to those people in that office. Sorry lady!

Around this time some of our relatives had got into tracing the Crump family tree, and they'd come up with quite a remarkable story. They went back as far as our great-great great-grandfather, who was born in a place called Burwash in Sussex, in 1768. He was called William Cramp.

His grandson, also William Cramp, emigrated to Maryborough, Queensland, in the early 1870s. He was a bush-man, a timber-getter, they called them in those days. He had a son called William Robert Cramp.

On the 25th of May, 1884, William Cramp and a mate of his called Thomas Crump attempted to cross an uncompleted rail-way bridge over a gully at Maryborough. Cramp fell sixty feet and was killed.

Eighteen months after that Thomas Crump married William Cramp's widow and she took the name of Crump. Our grandfa-ther, William Robert Cramp, who was then five years old, became a Crump, though he was not a blood relative of Thomas Crump.

Our father, Walter William Crump, was born in Auckland in 1908. I was born in Papatoe in 1935, and registered as John Barrie Crump.

The way I read all that it makes my actual name John Barrie Cramp. It's a good thing it doesn't matter one way or the other. Could be a hell of a tangle to sort out from here on.

The Toyota ad we'd done was proving quite popular. It had also won 'Commercial of the Year,' a 'Clio Recognition Award' and a Facts Award in Australia. They were bringing out a new model and got Scotty and me to make another TV ad.

These ads consisted mainly of me and Scotty booting a ute a bit fast around bush tracks with some clever dialogue, but somehow they had a bit of magic to them. The second one was popular too, and also won awards. Axis-New Zealand; Facts-Australia; Gold in the US Mobius, and a Silver Lion at Cannes. I don't know what all that means, I got the info from our mates at Colenso. Sounds impressive, eh!

We'd had a letter from the people we'd rented the shack off near Opotiki. They'd decided to sell their land and felt that we should have it. We replied saying thanks but it was out of the question, we never saw that kind of money. Then two things happened at once.

By this time my image was pretty tangled up with Toyota utes, and the Toyota people started paying me a retainer not to advertise anybody else's stuff. I wouldn't have anyway, but I was earning the money. Every time I stuck my head outside someone would come up and ask me how we did such-and such in our ads. I couldn't knock off, whenever I was in public I found myself talking Toyota, saying the same things to this person as I'd just been saying to someone else a few minutes ago. I could tell when they'd been running the commercials on television because even more unlikely people would come up and ask if I actually did the driving in the ads, or did we wreck any vehicles, where was my mate Scotty, what were those utes really like? Hard to maintain cordiality sometimes. It made it easier to handle now we were being paid for it. The Toyota people and their advertising agency, Colenso, have always been good to deal with and work with, and I've learned a great deal from our association.

The publicity I was getting had introduced me to a new generation of New Zealanders. The young people. They started reading my books, and liked them. There's no sex or violence or bad language in my writing and my books had been made recommended reading in the schools. I was already getting quite a bit of mail from people wanting me to speak at functions and conferences, Lions, Rotary, Lionesses, Chambers of Commerce, Christmas breakups, sendoffs, reunions, debates – you name it. And now schools and writers' classes were added to the list. I suppose every well-known person has their own way of saying no to people without offending them. If you tell them you're busy on that date they might just shift their dates to suit you. "I'll be away on a filming job during that month." "I'll be out of the country." "I'll have to get in touch with my agent, who's been away in the South Island/Australia." "I might have to go and give a mate of mine a hand on his fishing boat down at Port Jackson this winter." "Too much chance of me having to let you down at the last minute . . ." The truth of it is that I'm not ambitious enough to enjoy public performances. I just don't happen to like them, and I only ever speak in public when I'm cornered into it, usually through some other commitment.

The other thing that happened around the same time as we started getting payments from Toyota was that we got another letter from the people with the land near Opotiki. Were we absolutely sure we didn't want their place, before they sold it to someone else? We had a yarn about it. I'd never owned any house or land or anything, neither had Robyn. We decided it might be a good adventure. We'd have to borrow, and neither of us was up to mortgages and stuff, wouldn't have known where to start. If we owed two bucks we worried about it until it was paid back.

We finally arranged to borrow the money we needed from our friends and bought eleven acres of scrub and second growth with a one-room shack on it. We were landowners.

So here I was into my fifties before I knew what it was like to pay rates and bills and stuff like that. All I'd ever paid was cash for things and rent, and not a hell of a lot of that. I'd never owned anything before that I couldn't carry or drive away in.

We trapped possum-skins to get money. By this time I couldn't bring myself to slaughter a possum caught in a trap if I could avoid it, so Robyn trapped them and killed them and I did the skins. She didn't mind that arrangement in the least. We started breaking our eleven acres in by fencing and goats, as we could afford posts and wire.

I wrote a book I was quite pleased with, *Wild Pork and Watercress*, and it paid off everything we owed. Then Robyn and I split up. After putting up with more of me than anyone else ever has, she'd had enough. We squared-up and she took off to live a more normal kind of existence.

I carried on working on the place. Then I did a stint as cook for a merino-mustering gang in Otago and wrote a book called *Bullock Creek*. With the money from that book I bought the eleven-acre block next door to mine with the old woolshed and homestead on it. I now owned a twenty-two-acre sheep station, mostly in manuka and fern and blackberry. I'm working on it. A good way to keep fit.

I have fifty goats, twenty-two merino sheep (I like them), two horses, two dogs, two cats, nine chooks and a rooster, and two ducks. They've all got names but I won't burden you with them. That's ninety animals I'm responsible for, and all this gear. How did this happen? I seem to be settling down or something. If I am it'll be the biggest adventure yet, but it's a bit hard to believe that.

I've still got my sack of possum-traps out in the shed, I could have the ute loaded and be away from here in less than half an hour. I know exactly what to take, and in spite of the fact that the ute seems to start champing at the winch every time we get out near the main road I'm not in any great hurry. Life's not bad here yet.

These days, apart from working on my place, I do a bit of river rafting, ride around on my horse, some photography (put out a calendar in 1989 called *Humble Abodes*), some fishing, some TV and radio work, setting up to play a leading role in a feature film being made out of one of my books (that'll be a challenge!), the occasional conference (where I cut my way into the conference-room with a chainsaw, tell a joke and then scarper), some in-house video and voiceover work, occasional television commercials (mainly for Toyota), and the few public appearances I can't avoid, but writing is what I like doing best.

In 1990 I was honoured by some of my writing being included in Frank Muir's *Oxford Book of Humorous Prose*, along with authors such as Caxton, Dickens, Lamb, Trollope, Lear, Mark Twain, Thurber, Wodehouse and many more of those writers I've admired all my life. It's a bit hard to believe.

I must say it's only as I look through what I've written in this book that I realise how much courage some of my women have had. The smart ones gave up on me early on, but the few that stuck it out hung on through more than you'd expect, just looking at them. I've known plenty of men who'd have chucked it in long before they did. I suppose it's a bit like finding out if a bloke's going to be any good as a deer-culler. You can't tell until you've had 'em out in the scrub for a while.

Look at Jean, a psychology student and delicate intellectual flower from the academic fringes of Auckland, quoting T.S. Elliot at poetry-readings and scrawling notes on paper serviettes for a short story she was writing about smells in coffee-bars – staggering down the Paringa riverbed in front of me in the rain, the blood from the stag she was carrying dripping down the backs of her skinny legs; clinging to the saddle, only her head and the horse's visible above the water as they got swept down the flooded Mahitahi and only just made it across;

holding the harpoon for me as we paddle through a mangrove swamp at night in a cloud of mosquitoes, hundreds of miles from the nearest human habitation, looking for bigger crocodiles; sitting in the hatchway of the *Waterwitch* beside me in a screaming gale and thirty-foot waves, unable to turn aside until the storm subsided or we went up on the reef; standing on a washed-up log looking for boats when she knew bloody well that no boats were going to come and we were all going to die.

And after years of that she ups and off into the Red Heart of Australia with a bunch of strangers to look for Lassitter's Lost Reef. And all the gutsy things in between.

And Robyn, just twenty-one and looking at the most sixteen. She'd already saved up and travelled on her own around a lot of the world, living on a trailbike and grooving around New Zealand. Going off with an old broke bushman and living in the open and sleeping in the back of a Model-A, in winter, in Rough Creek. She knows what it's like to be cold, Robyn does. Carrying me across the creek to save me getting my feet wet and prove she can do it (She's only as big as thruppence, I wrote a book called *Shorty* once to try and make her see how unimportant being short is), and off round her traps in a pair of high-heeled boots we'd found in the Hokitika rubbish-tip because we couldn't buy her any boots until we sold some skins.

Then three months down the Black River without seeing a house or shop or a road or another woman. That'd rock most people. Whited-out in a snowstorm on our trapline in Otago prodding ahead with a stick because the edge is just over there somewhere and if we don't find the track down we'll die up here. Riding back into our claim over the Moonlight Trail, iced-up and pitch dark. Too dangerous to try and steer your horse, or lead the pack-horse, who kept stopping to eat and then trotting to catch up and breaking all the candles and eggs.

190

Robyn never jibbed at anything and she never complained. The only thing I ever knew her to give up on was me, and I don't blame her for that.

And all my other wives and women and mothers of my nine sons. I must be a bastard to live with, but I hope I've been good value along the way. I've got no complaints about life, I've had a pretty good innings so far.

Another thing I realise from looking back over what I've written here is that I've actually done the things I read about and dreamed of doing when I was a boy on the farm. I've climbed the mountains and hunted the deer and the boar. I've lived in the bush and run trap-lines for my living, and been in blizzards and floods. I've harpooned the big saurian from the prow of my little boat. I know what it's like to be shipwrecked and nearly die of thirst, and to be marooned on a tropical island. I've travelled through strange lands and lived with people on the other side of the world. I've paddled canoes through steaming tropical jungles and dived in a coral lagoon and ridden a giant turtle out across the reef. It's a bit strange to think I did all that and then wrote it down without realising it was the fulfilment of vivid childhood dreams.

I don't know how much I've changed during all this, but I do notice that the hand that once drove the harpoon into the neck of the big saltwater crocodile, now reaches down to pluck aside a worm before I ram my posthole.

Well that's my story up to date, the way I seen it. It was real interesting to write it down on the pages and I hope you've enjoyed reading it.

Aroha!

Johnny Cramp

Pakihi Valley

October 1991

191

Song of a Drifter

I've cut me load, and that's me song,
It's time I hit the track,
I've been round here for far too long
And now I'm headin' back.

I'm splittin' from this worn-out scene,
I'm packin' up me gear,
I'm takin' off for pastures green,
I'm snatchin' it from here.

I've heard the things they said to me,
I've bogged meself in stuff,
I've took responsibility
And now I've had enough.

I'll drag me hook, I'll just un-front,
I'm headin' for the door,
I'm castin' off, I'll pole me punt,
I'm not here any more.

So good luck, mate, I'm movin' on,
I'll leave the place to you,
And if they ask you where I've gone
Just tell them I shot through.

And if we meet some other place
A stranger you will be,
I can't remember name or face,
They're all the same to me.

I'll greet you like a brother,
I'll make you laugh somehow,
And then one day I'll drift away,
Just like I'm doin' now.